PEARLS FROM
THE PROPHET
EZEKIEL

BIBLE STUDY AIDS *of William G. Heslop*

PEARLS FROM THE PROPHET EZEKIEL

by
William G. Heslop, D.D., Litt. S.D.

KREGEL PUBLICATIONS
Grand Rapids, Michigan 49501

Library of Congress Catalog Card Number: 76-12081
ISBN 0-8254-2832-7

Kregel Publications edition 1976
Reprinted 1983

Printed in the United States of America

CONTENTS

FOREWORD

This exposition of Ezekiel is a companion volume to "Gems from Genesis," "Riches from Revelation," "Diamonds from Daniel," "Nuggets from Numbers," and "Gold from the Gospels." Ezekiel, whose name means "God will strengthen" was a priest as well as a prophet. He grew up amidst the changes which the good Josiah had introduced. In the year 597 B.C. Nebuchadnezzer took Jerusalem and carried into captivity the king and the best of the people, Ezekiel among them. There is no serious doubt that Ezekiel wrote his great prophetic book. The whole contents are a "thus saith the Lord." In view of the present conflict between the TOTALITARIAN states and the DEMOCRATIC states, a conflict between the forces of FETTERS and of those who believe in FREEDOM, it is most interesting and instructive to note that EZEKIEL clearly foretold the final defeat of Germany, Italy and also later that of Russia. Ezekiel 38 and 39 clearly teaches that Italy must lose both Ethiopia and Libya and while no dates are given this may well prove the day of reckoning for the blasphemous Mussolini. According to Ezekiel RUSSIA, with Persia, ETHIOPIA and LIBYA, is to make a savage onslaught against Palestine which is now nursed and protected by Great Britain. Russia is to be finally overthrown for God Almighty is against her (38:2). The defeat and overthrow of Germany, Italy and finally Russia is clearly foreshadowed in EZEKIEL 38-39. In view of the present conflict with all its attendant evils and dangers the Book of Ezekiel is of special importance to us all today.

PART ONE

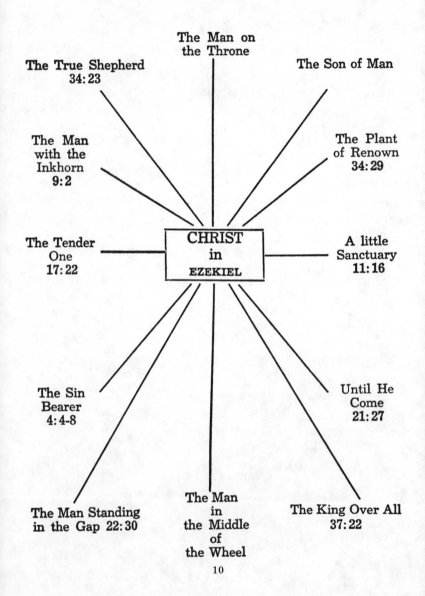

The Man on
the Throne

The True Shepherd
34:23

The Son of Man

The Man
with the
Inkhorn
9:2

The Plant
of Renown
34:29

The Tender
One
17:22

CHRIST
in
EZEKIEL

A little
Sanctuary
11:16

The Sin
Bearer
4:4-8

Until He
Come
21:27

The Man Standing
in the Gap 22:30

The Man
in
the Middle
of
the Wheel

The King Over All
37:22

10

The Book of Ezekiel

1. **AUTHOR**

   Ezekiel (1) The son of Buzi
   (2) A prophet and a priest
   (3) A captive

2. **DATE**

   593 to 566 B.C.

3. **PLACE**

   Tel-abib, among the captives, by the river of Chebar in Babylon.

4. **PURPOSE**

   (1) To warn of coming doom
   (2) Promise of coming deliverance

5. **MESSIANIC IDEAS**

   (1) Son of man
   (2) The man on and above the throne
   (3) The man with the inkhorn
   (4) Man to stand in the gap
   (5) The man in the middle of the wheel
   (6) A plant of renown
   (7) The true Shepherd
   (8) The King over all

Call and Commission of Ezekiel

Ezekiel began his ministry in the fifth year of Jehoiachin's captivity.

In Daniel and Ezekiel there is given a full revelation of the plans and purposes of God for Israel and the world.

Ezekiel was both a priest and a prophet to the people of God.

The hand of the Lord was upon him in both receiving and declaring the messages of Jehovah.

These messages were not only intended for a few exiles at Chebar, but for all Israel and for all time.

Ezekiel entered on his prophetic mission about the year 594 B.C. He labored for over twenty years, concluding his prophecies with a glowing description of Israel's glory in the latter days.

The Book of Ezekiel may be divided into three parts:

1. Testimonies against Israel and Jerusalem, chapters 1-24.

2. Judgments against the surrounding nations, chapters 25-32.

3. Future restoration and glory of Israel, chapters 33-48.

EZEKIEL

Scripture	Exposition
Ezekiel	"Whom God strengthens."
The captives	The people of God.
The whirlwind	Sowing the wind, they were about to reap the Whirlwind.
Fire	The Divine Presence.
The living creature	Christ.
Four living creatures	Four characters of Christ.
Likeness of man	Jesus.
Wings	Swift.
Eyes	Intelligence, omniscience.
One wheel	The whole plan and purpose of God.
Four wheels	The providences of God, the distinct purposes of God in His dealings with all mankind.
A throne	Judgment.
A man on the throne	Jesus Christ.
The bow	Mercy.
Lion	Strength.
Ox	Endurance, patience.
Man	Intelligence.
Eagle	Vision, swiftness.

THE WORD OF THE LORD

EZEKIEL 1

The word of the Lord came expressly unto Ezekiel
   (1:3).

Ezekiel was a captive and in the land of the
stranger. God opened heaven and gave him visions
and revelations of His word and will. The hour of
greatest need is the hour of the Divine Presence,
and Divine Strength. In the most hopeless hour of
life, in the darkest and dreariest days, in the loneli-
est moments of human miseries, God will be at hand
to strengthen and save.

The world which clubbed Abel and mocked
Noah, jeered at Isaac, flung the Hebrews into a hot
fire, and doomed Daniel to a den of lions, may throw
its Ezekiels into lonely captivity, but while they bind
the prophet and preacher, they cannot bind the
Word of God. Hence, "The word . . . came expressly unto Ezekiel."

God's ministers and people may be bound but
the Word of God and Spirit of God cannot be
bound. Rome may imprison its Paul, but it could
not imprison the truth. John may be placed upon

a lonely isle, but the riches of the Book of Revelation shall find its way around the world.

God's minister may be taken captive and bound but the word of God is free. Paul may be beheaded, but his inspired letters are borne on every breeze. John may be imprisoned but the truths he pens shall prevail and prosper.

This verse drops the guillotine on the neck of the gullible critics. These self-styled and so-called higher critics claim that Ezekiel was a close student of Jeremiah for years and that before writing, the mind of the Prophet Ezekiel had been saturated with the ideas and language of Jeremiah. Other critics have accused Ezekiel of mental abnormality and have stated that he was subject to a form of catalepsy—a psychical subject—taken to trances— and a clairvoyant. What mad things can be invented by critics who claim unusual scholarship in order to get rid of unwelcome truth. Such ridiculous ravings require no answer. "The word of the Lord came expressly unto Ezekiel." If Ezekiel was a cataleptic then good Lord give us some more cataleptics. I could wish for a cataleptic fit right now, if the prophecy of Ezekiel was thus produced.

"The word of the Lord came expressly unto Ezekiel the priest, the son of Buzi, in the land of the Chaldeans by the river Chebar; and the hand of the Lord was there upon him."

The name Ezekiel means "The Strength of God," "God Will Strengthen," or "Strengthened by God."

God's calls are His enablings. The whole ministry of the Prophet is characterized by strength and courage. He stood like a giant refreshed with new wine against the wilfulness and wickedness of the Jews and against the pride and cruelty of the Chaldeans. He threw himself impassionately and unselfishly against the sins of his own people and his own times.

The hand of the Lord was there upon him (1:3).

Four things are clearly mentioned by Ezekiel, the author of the book: (1) The heavens were opened; (2) he saw visions of God; (3) The word of the Lord came unto him, and (4) the hand of the Lord was upon him. An open heaven, a present God, a distinct revelation, and ability to perform.

This remarkable expression occurs seven times.

(1) 1:3, "The word of the Lord came expressly unto Ezekiel the priest, the son of Buzi, in the land of the Chaldeans by the river Chebar; and the hand of the Lord was there upon him."

(2) 3:14, "So the spirit lifted me up, and took me away, and I went in bitterness, in the heat of my spirit; but the hand of the Lord was strong upon me."

(3) 3:22, "And the hand of the Lord was there upon me."

(4) 8:1, "And it came to pass in the sixth year, in the sixth month, in the fifth day of the month, as I sat in mine house, and the elders of Judah sat

before me, that the hand of the Lord GOD fell there upon me."

(5) 33:22, "Now the hand of the Lord was upon me in the evening."

(6) 37:1, "The hand of the Lord was upon me, and carried me out in the spirit of the Lord, and set me down in the midst of the valley which was full of dry bones."

(7) 40:1, "In the five and twentieth year of our captivity, in the beginning of the year; in the tenth day of the month, in the fourteenth year after the city was smitten, in the selfsame day the hand of the Lord was upon me, and brought me thither."

The power of God took hold of Ezekiel and produced this great book and prophecy.

The hand of the Lord was there upon Ezekiel.

1. The Hand of God.

The *Word* of God and the *Hand* of God.

The Word to reveal, and the Hand to empower.

The Word to tell us what to do and where to go and the Hand to enable us and strengthen us in the path of obedience.

The Word (truth) and the Hand (power).

The Word for instruction and the Hand for grace and strength.

The Word of God for wisdom and understanding and the Hand of the Lord for obedience in everyday life. The Word and the Hand.

Obey the Word and you will feel the Hand!

2. *There upon Ezekiel.*

There, in the darkness and loneliness.

There, among unbelievers and strangers.

There, despite the hopelessness and distress.

There, passing through an apparently endless tunnel, the hand of God was *there* upon Ezekiel and the same hand can be felt upon us.

Visions of God.

Isaiah's *vision of God* revealed to him the sinfulness of his own people and his own need of the fiery baptism with the Holy Ghost. It also made known to him the necessity for making Holiness known to others. He heard the call and offered himself for service. Holiness and then power. Personal sanctification and then service.

Peter's *vision of God* was given in order to convince him that holiness was for all men irrespective of race, color, nationality, election, language, preference, or predestination.

Paul's *vision of God* put an end to his self-righteous Phariseeism and transformed him into the flaming holiness warrior and missionary of Christ.

Ezekiel's *vision of God* unveiled the story of Israel's time of trouble, and also the ultimate deliverance and blessing under Christ their King.

These men saw things clearly, for a man of vision is a man who "sees before others see, sees more than others see, and sees more clearly than others see."

A man above upon it (1:26).

The Book of Ezekiel is a book full of encouragements to the troubled saints. It is a book for the times. Like the Book of Revelation, it has to do with things which shall come to pass. Both these Apocalyptic books are beacon lights sending their benign and beneficent rays against the background of the church's apostasy and backslidings. Both books look forward to the full and final establishment of the kingdom of Christ. Looking down the centuries, both John and Ezekiel link arms and look with a single eye upon the unfolding of God's gracious plans for His people.

The MAN in the middle of the Wheel.

There is *a man* at the center of this wheel. There is *a man* in the center of these wheels. There is *a man* at the hub of these wheels within a wheel and that man is *the man,* the Lord Jesus Christ. The seed of the woman in Genesis is the man in the middle of the wheel in Ezekiel. The Passover lamb in Exodus is the man at the hub of the wheels in Ezekiel. The man of sorrows in Isaiah is the man of triumph in the center of the wheels within the wheel in the Book of Ezekiel.

The *eyes* are the eyes of the omniscient Son of man and Son of God. The *lion* is the lion of the tribe of Judah. The *ox* is the patient Sufferer of Calvary. The *eagle* is the heavenly One come down to earth. The *man* is the Man of Galilee.

The heavens were opened.

The heavens were opened to Moses, Stephen and the Lord Jesus Christ. Opened heavens are also promised to faithful, systematic tithers. In a foreign land, a captive, living among enemies, realizing and in a measure bearing the sins of his own people, Ezekiel saw the glory of God by direct inspiration and revelation and made it known to others.

Four living creatures.

Four is the number for humanity. These four living ones typify *redeemed* humanity. In the Book of Revelation they sing a song of praise for the redemption of man. These four living creatures lead the host of humanity in singing, praising and worshiping. *The face of man* speaks of their being *intelligent,* wise and knowing living ones, thus distinguishing them from the brute creation, which have *instinct* but no wisdom or intelligence.

The face of a lion sets forth the quality of *courage,* bravery and fearlessness, the righteous being as bold as a lion.

The face of an ox or calf, represents the grace of patience, and willingness in pulling loads and carrying burdens, *ready for service or sacrifice.* *The face of an eagle* deals with their *vision,* farsightedness, power of flight, ability to ride above the storm, outride the storm and even soar above it, thus making the storm serve its purpose and pleasure. The eagle is a bird of the heavens. These are all qualities and characteristics of New Testament saints. They are *intelligent* and wise. They have sense enough to keep in tune with their infinite Creator and Redeemer and being wise shall shine as the brightness of the firmament. *They are courageous.* Neither popes, priests nor prelates can compel or persuade them to compromise their convictions, trifle with conscience or tinker with the truth of God. Neither fagots, furnaces, nor fires can either frighten them or make them give up their faith. They prefer a martyr's death and a martyr's crown rather than deny the Christ who redeemed them.

They are pullers of loads and carriers of burdens and they are ready for either service or sacrifice. If the loads are too heavy to pull while standing on their feet they will drop down on their knees and pull or die in the attempt.

They are far-sighted, they look off and away from the things that are temporal, vanishing and passing, and look up to the things which are eternal. Their affections are set and centered on things which are above. The storms of life are used to nestle them closer to the heart of God. The qualities and characteristics of the living creatures are qualities and characteristics of the redeemed saints. The other features, too, of these living creatures are interesting and instructive. "Eyes before and behind," intimates that they understand the future (before) and the past (behind). All is now clear and plain.

"Wings" denote a higher and wider sphere of service stretching out before these redeemed and glorified saints.

The four living creatures thus not only set forth four characters of Christ but typify redeemed and glorified saints.

THE FOUR LIVING CREATURES

Ezekiel 1-3

Scripture	Exposition
"And I looked"	Look off and look up.
"and behold,"	Attention, please.
"a whirlwind,"	Sudden wrath, no more warnings, exhortations, or calls to repentance.
"came out of the north,"	from the direction of Babylon.
"and a fire infolding itself,"	Christ, like the sun, is a fire infolding itself.
"the colour of amber,"	Golden and fiery. A picture of Christ in judgment.
"Four living creatures,"	Representatives and leaders of redeemed humanity.
"the likeness of a man,"	Uprightness, reason, wisdom and intelligence.
"four faces,"	Understanding of all things in every direction.
"four wings,"	Heavenly, glorified and swift.
"straight feet,"	Holy walk, holy progress.
"like a calf's,"	Clean.
"like . . . burnished brass,"	Unyielding and unbending righteousness and justice.
"and they had the hands of a man,"	Usefulness, fellowship.
"their wings were joined one to another,"	Unity in action.
""they turned not,"	Unlike Lot's wife in the Old Testament, and Demas in

the New, they neither turned around nor back. With glorified bodies they go straight, in any and every direction. With *straight* feet they go straight forward.

"they four"
Unity, oneness.

"had the face of a man"
Reason, intelligence, wisdom and knowledge.

"the face of a lion"
Courage, boldness, majesty, strength, fearlessness.

"the face of an ox"
Patiently pulling loads, carrying burdens and ready for service.

"the face of an eagle"
Vision, powerful in flight, swift to rise above the earth and things of earth.

"their wings were stretched upward"
Not folded as though they were taking things easy, but ready to go in any direction at any time.

"stretched upward"
Forward (9) and upward (11).

"two covered their bodies"
They are clothed. All in heaven are clothed, as all in hell are nude. Nudism was born in hell. It is not back to nature, for all animals are clothed. It is *down* to barbarism and hell.

"whither the spirit was to go, they went";
Heavenly direction and guidance from within and without. They know the mind of the Spirit and work in harmony. All in

"their appearance was like burning coals of fire"

heaven are in harmony. Bright, burning, and shining.

"and like the appearance of lamps"

Light giving as well as shining.

"it went up and down among the living creatures"

Streaks of light and fire emanate from their glorified bodies. (1) Up, (2) Down, (3) Among.

"and the living creatures ran and returned"

Diligence, earnestness, zeal. Going and returning to their appointed p l a c e s, ready for further service. They do quickly that which must be done and then back to receive new orders.

"as the appearance of a flash of lightning"

Swift, implicit, unquestioning obedience.

These qualities and characteristics are now germinal in all believers. They will be perfected and completed in glorification.

"behold one *wheel* upon the earth"

The wheels set forth the goings of God.

"the wheels like unto the color of a beryl"

Green.

"their work, as it were a wheel in the middle of a wheel"

It is always difficult to describe the things of one country in the language of another.

A wheel in the middle of a wheel is an attempt to set forth *the strange ways of God* in the language of earth.

"as for their rings they . . . were dreadful"	These wheels as they go and their rims as they speed on, seem to cut a swath so large that it seemed too much to describe.
"full of eyes"	They see in all directions, everything is open, plain and clear.
"the wheels were lifted up"	These wheels, their motions and their appearances set forth the restless and irresistible course of God's power.
"for the spirit of the living creature was in the wheels."	The spirit of life, fire, power, glory and grandeur which was within the living creature also possessed the wheels. All alike were filled with God. All alike were God possessed and God controlled.
"when those went"	The living creatures.
"these went"	The wheels.
"and when those stood"	The living creatures.
"these stood."	The wheels.
	The providential goings of God ceased when the living creatures stopped.
	Judgment began with and ended with these living creatures.
"as . . . the terrible crystal"	Insufferably brilliant, as the blazing sun on the shining snow on a January morning. As insufferably bright as a thousand electric

	lights flashed suddenly upon the eye at midnight.
"as the . . . crystal"	Shining and transparent.
"the likeness of a throne"	A throne speaks of judgment.
"a man above upon it"	(1) A man (Christ)
	(2) Upon it (the throne)
	(3) Above (everyone and everything is under Christ). Christ is above all.
"the appearance of fire"	Our God is a consuming fire.

This chapter gives a symbolico-typical word picture of (1) the Lord Jesus Christ and (2) His redeemed, glorified, raptured saints, exalted, *judging and governing,* enshrouded in grandeur and glory.

Lamentations, and mourning, and woe (2: 10).

Ezekiel had seen a symbolical foreshadowing of Christ with His redeemed saints exalted, judging, reigning and ruling, supreme. Having seen things most difficult to express and explain in the language of humans the prophet was so overcome that he fell upon his face. Down in the dust in weakness of body and humility of heart he was ordered to stand upon his feet. God's commands are always His enablings and hence the Holy Spirit fills the prophet—seer—priest and set him upon his feet. The *command* to *stand* was immediately followed by the *power* to *stand* and Ezekiel, sanctified and unctionized, was thus made ready for further revelations. He was to go to the rebellious house of Israel. He was to speak to the impudent, stiff-necked and hard-hearted children of Israel. He was to receive (open his mouth), appropriate and assimilate (and eat that I give thee) the truth and without fear or favor deliver it to the people. The message was to be a message of judgment. The cup of their iniquity was full. The line between God's mercy and His wrath had been crossed and hence there was left nothing but judgment. "There was written therein lamentations, mourning, and woe."

The spirit lifted me up (3:14).

  (1) The spirit entered into me (2:2).

  (2) The spirit took me up (3:12).

  (3) The spirit lifted me up (3:14).

Ezekiel was Spirit possessed, Spirit moved, Spirit filled and Spirit controlled.

He called on the Spirit to come and breathe on the dry, yea, very dry bones.

He reassures his people that Jehovah will put His Spirit within them.

He testifies that the Spirit not only entered him, moved him and lifted him, but came mightily upon him and spake through him.

He foreshadowed a coming day when Jews and Gentiles would be honored by a pentecostal visitation. "Be filled with the Spirit."

I sat ... astonished ... seven days (3:15).

Having received, appropriated and assimilated the truth which was as honey for sweetness, for

God's truth is always sweet to the taste of God's people, Ezekiel was taken up by the Spirit to deliver the message to his own people of the captivity at Tel-abib by the River Chebar. The prophet felt the full force of the storm which was about to break over the heads of the sinful and haughty house of Israel. He saw their sad condition and felt their rebellious spirit and with the word of God burning in his heart, he sat speechless for seven days. He *acted* as though the storm had already passed and they were dead (v. 15). "Then I came to them of the captivity at Tel-abib, that dwelt by the river of Chebar, and I sat where they sat, and remained there astonished among them seven days."

He shall die in his sin (3:20).

The theory of "eternal sonship" and "once in grace always in grace" here receives its knock-down, knock-out, death blow. In four simple, clear and plain verses the Holy Spirit declares the possibility of a righteous man turning from his righteousness . . . committing iniquity and dying in his sin. Not only may a holy man turn from the ways of holiness and commit sin, but all his past life of goodness, righteousness, holiness and service shall not be remembered (v. 20). "Again, when a righteous man doth turn away from his righteousness, and commit iniquity, and I lay a stumblingblock before him, he shall die, because thou hast not given him warning, he shall die in his sin, and his righteousness which he hath done shall not be remembered, but his blood will I require at thine hand." There can be no appeal from this plain passage of scripture. The question is settled. The debate is closed.

PART TWO
Judgments Against Jerusalem
SIGNS AND SYMBOLS, TYPES AND SHADOWS

THE SIGN OF THE TILE

"Thou also, son of man, take thee a tile and lay it before thee, and pourtray upon it the city, even Jerusalem. And lay siege against it, and build a fort against it, and cast a mount against it; set the camp also against it, and set battering rams against it round about. Moreover, take thou unto thee an iron pan, and set it for a wall of iron between thee and the city; and set thy face against it, and it shall be besieged, and thou shalt lay siege against it. This shall be a sign to the house of Israel."

Ezekiel does not by long exordium or preamble beg our attention. He demands it. Trumpets do not blow out apologies. They send forth battle blasts and war sounds.

Historically speaking Ezekiel was a captive but religiously speaking he was wondrously free.

Daniel was freer in the den of lions than Darius was on the throne.

The three holy Hebrews were far freer in the fiery furnace than was Nebuchadnezzar as he glared into the flames and saw the Form of the Fourth in the midst.

Bunyan in the so-called prison produced the "Pilgrim's Progress." There is no prison for men like Bunyan, Peter or Paul.

The sons of God cannot be bounded by four walls. The size of one's house depends on the size of the heart. If someone in our day were to say that he had received a vision of God such as Ezekiel saw, he would be considered a fool.

We blatantly boast of our practical common sense and leave out the visions of God. We have lost much by our lack of visions of God.

We need to get back to a few more peeps into Paradise above.

We need to be made conscious of the larger life, higher glory and bigger world. We should not consent to live unblessed by heavenly visions and heavenly visitants.

SCRIPTURE	EXPOSITION
"Take thee a tile"	A tile blackboard about two feet long, and a foot broad and four inches thick.
"and pourtray upon it the city"	Teaching by pictures (a pictorial sermon).
"set battering rams against it"	A long beam with head of brass and catapulted against the walls. Thus the coming siege was portrayed by the prophet.
"an iron pan"	A large flat plate.
"set it for a wall of iron"	Sign of Israel's (1) Separation from God and (2) Protection for the prophet.

4

THE SIGN OF THE PROSTRATE PROPHET

Ezekiel 4

4 Lie thou also upon thy left side, and lay the iniquity of the house of Israel upon it: according to the number of the days that thou shalt lie upon it thou shalt bear their iniquity.

5 For I have laid upon thee the years of their iniquity, according to the number of the days, three hundred and ninety days: so shalt thou bear the iniquity of the house of Israel.

6 And when thou hast accomplished them, lie again on thy right side, and thou shalt bear the iniquity of the house of Judah forty days: I have appointed thee each day for a year.

7 Therefore thou shalt set thy face toward the siege of Jerusalem, and thine arm shall be uncovered, and thou shalt prophesy against it.

8 And, behold, I will lay bands upon thee, and thou shalt not turn thee from one side to another, till thou hast ended the days of thy siege.

Scripture	Exposition
"Lie thou . . . upon thy left side"	As of one crushed to the ground, prostrate under a burden.
"thou shalt bear their iniquity"	Type of Christ as the sin bearer (substitution).

"three hundred and ninety days." 390 years of sorrow, shame and suffering for the house of Israel.

"lie again on thy right side . . . forty days." Forty years of punishment for the house of Judah.

"I will lay bands upon thee" Both Israel and Judah were to be helpless and hopeless under the heels of the oppressor. Sin ends in sorrow, suffering, sighing, shame and slavery.

5

THE SIGN OF THE FAMINE

EZEKIEL 4

SCRIPTURE

"Take thou also unto thee wheat . . . by weight"

"drink also water by measure and thou shalt bake it with dung that cometh out of man in their sight."

"even thus shall the children of Israel eat their defiled bread among the Gentiles."

EXPOSITION

The exceeding sinfulness of sin in the sight of Jehovah is here set forth by this action picture of the prophet. How disgusting and revolting it must have appeared to this holy man of God, to stoop to kneading dough while mixing it with the dung of man. Thus is set forth the unclean, polluting, defiling effects of disobedience.

What a sickening sight it must have been to contemplate *making* bread with man's dung. What a far more sickening sight to see the Chosen People of God *eating* such bread. And what a pitiable, painful ordeal it must have been to thus make and eat such polluted bread *among the Gentiles*.

Thus is portrayed the degrading results of disobedience to God and God's Word.

We should learn that it is less defiling and polluting to eat dung than it is to disobey God. Sin is the most defiling and costly thing in the Universe.

"cow's dung for man's dung"
The horrified p r o p h e t pleaded his own cause before the just Judge of all the earth and received a measure of respite but it was only a measure.

"they shall eat bread by weight and with care"
Famine stalking through the land . . . cheerfulness departed because God had forsaken them.

"for their iniquity"
Not because Jehovah did not love them nor had not chosen them, *but for their iniquity*. Their own evil deeds and departure from God spelled *death*. "That they may consume away for their iniquity."

These actions and signs were symbolic testimonies to the house of Israel. The interpretation of the eating of coarse and polluted bread is given in vs. 16, 17. "Moreover, he said unto me, Son of man, behold I will break the staff of bread in Jerusalem, and they shall eat bread by weight and with care, and they shall drink water by measure, and with astonishment. That they may want bread and water, and be astonished one with another, and consume away for their iniquity."

In the East the dung of animals is used for fuel, as wood is scarce. To use either the dung of man or animals to prepare bread implies the most awful need and pollution. It also implied that in the sight of God the nation had dropped to the level of the heathen and that the abominable preparing of bread with dung was less hateful than the sins of which they were all guilty. To sin against God is much worse than eating either the dung of the cow or the dung of man.

6

THE SIGN OF THE SHARP KNIFE
AND BARBER'S RAZOR

EZEKIEL 5-8

Keys which unlock the Bible are usually found within its pages. The *sharp knife* and *barber's razor* were the kings of Assyria and Babylon. The *hair* shaven from the head and beard, and divided, represented the *people*. One-third of the people were to be burned with fire, one-third slain with the sword and one-third scattered. The "balances" express God's careful discrimination even in the outpourings of His wrath. The *few* hairs to be bound in the prophet's robes represent the remnant who would escape but the sword would follow them. To think that such would come upon Jerusalem the city of the great King. The sword still follows the Jews and the city is still defiled by the feet of Gentiles.

"Take thee a sharp knife, take thee a barber's razor"	The kings of Assyria and Babylon.
"cause . . . to pass upon thine head and . . . beard"	The hair of his head and beard represent the people of Israel and Judah.
"take thee balances"	God weighs all people in just balances.
"divide the hair"	The people.
"burn with fire a third part"	One-third of all the Chosen People were to be destroyed by fire.
"take a third part, and smite about it with a knife"	One-third to be slain with the sword.
"and a third part . . . scat-	One-third scattered and dis-

43

ter in the wind"
"and I will draw out a sword after them"

persed among the nations. Fulfilled to this very day. Even the dispersed and scattered remnant were to be persecuted, hated and followed by the sword. In Germany and Russia today life is unbearable and uncertain, as it is in many other places.

"take a few . . . and bind them in thy skirts"

A small remnant was to be saved and preserved despite the hatred of kings and nations. *One* word of *four* letters proves the inspiration, authenticity and veracity of the sacred Scriptures, and that word is JEWS.

2,500 years ago a few were to be preserved and they are still preserved. They can neither be annihilated, exterminated nor assimilated. God's Word is true and sure.

"then take of them again . . . and burn them in the fire"

Fire, flame, and sword were to follow the whole house of Israel because of their sins. Even the saved and preserved remnant would suffer, although preserved. They are suffering today.

V. 5 is the key to the whole.

"This is Jerusalem"

"This is Jerusalem."

7

THE END IS COME

An end, the end is come (7:22).

"Also thou son of man, thus saith the Lord God unto the land of Israel; An end, the end is come upon the four corners of the land."

"An end is come, the end is come: it watcheth for thee; behold, it is come." Every day has its sunset and every year has its December. There is an end to everything of earth, time and sense. There is an end to the day of pleasure and to the life of sin. There is an end to our life of indecision and half-hearted devotion. The day of God's vengeance is at hand. The voice of God cannot be mistaken. It is different. It startles.

The poet sees what the prosaic-minded person never apprehends. The painter beholds pictures impossible to the mind of the inartistic. The sculptor sees an angel or a demon in a block of marble. Just so, the man of visions, the man with God's hand upon him sees things which cannot be seen, and hears things which cannot be heard.

The carping, so-called higher critics, have seen in verse thirteen a very serious discrepancy. The inspired writer of the Book of Ezekiel is here supposed to be in error and caught in a self-contradiction. Zedekiah was to be taken to Babylon and was to die there *and yet not see it. How could a person* go to the beautiful city of Babylon, live and die there, and yet not see it? asks the contentious critics. This is simple, easy, plain as eating pie, answers the saint. His eyes were put out by Nebuchadnezzar before arriving in Babylon.

These heady and high-minded wise-crackers also profess to have found very serious mistakes in the writings of Moses, such as his statement that there was not a house in Egypt where there was not one dead. The destroying angel had visited the land of darkness and slain the firstborn in all Egypt. The critics contend that Israel was specially protected by Jehovah in Egypt and that in their houses there was no one slain. The answer here as elsewhere is simple. In every house in Egypt there was either a dead son or a dead lamb. "There was not a house in which there was not one dead."

The image of jealousy (8:3).

Trial for jealousy is set forth in the Book of Numbers. There are more idols in the world than there are human beings. Idols of all sizes and shapes and for all purposes under the sun. The writer has seen all kinds of idols and thousands of them for unimaginable and unspeakable purposes. This image of jealousy was one to which troubled and storm-tossed people prayed whose hearts and homes had been hurt by unfaithful companions. As ashes smother the flames in the furnace so jealousy smothers both love and sense.

It is the opposite to love for love demands faith.

Carnal jealousy is cruel. Unbridled passion leads to perdition. Justification and sanctification perfect the soul in love. Without the true God and without heart holiness man sets up his own gods and goes about to establish his own righteousness.

Man is religious and must bend and bow either to God or idols.

Hast thou . . . seen what the ancients . . . do in the dark? (8:12).

Sin shuns the light. The deeds of darkness are dreadful. If we could look within the breast of the unbeliever and ungodly we would behold a cage of unclean birds and beasts. Man has within him all the elements of the torments of hell. An accusing, condemning conscience hails him to the tribunal of justice and vengeance. The remembrance of past sin terrifies the unregenerate sons of men.

The tale of the goblet is true. There is a serpent in every cup of sinful pleasure. There is a stinging fly in all earthly ointment. Coiled for the spring and with gleaming eyes in its head, its fangs raised and ready to strike, the serpent of sin within smites the soul, damns the man and lands him in everlasting darkness.

A serpent lurks at the bottom of every selfish, sinful pleasure.

Deeds of darkness end in distress, death and damnation.

The chambers of his imagery (8:12).

This is a striking expression. It is an arresting sentence. It represents a man haunted with visionary presences on his way to hell. A man, who, because of sin, retires into himself, and has shut the door of his soul, and now beholds ghostly and ghastly scenes.

Portraits and pictures of the past presage sure and certain perdition for the future, as well as the present. Here is a man filled with forebodings of future ill as well as unspeakable impurities of the present. His secret sins and lusts have mastered and murdered his soul, and, deceived while he lives, he is damned when dead (v. 12, last clause).

Women weeping for Tammuz (8:14).

(1) Women (2) Weeping (3) Tammuz

These duped, deceived and deluded women were weeping because of the death of one of their innumerable gods.

People make gods of their own and weep because their self-made gods fail to save or help them.

At once the bane and blessing of mankind and the weepers of the world, it seems ten thousand pities that women are yet to be found who shed tears because of departed idols. Satan's attacks have always been against the womanhood of the world. The hand that rocks the cradle leads to the White House or to hell.

They worshipped the sun (8:16).

The abominations recorded in Ezekiel eight increase in violence and wickedness.

Greater than women weeping for Tammuz and greater than the evil churnings in the chambers of man's imagery and greater than the unspeakable and nameless sins committed by the ancients of the house of Israel in the dark and greater than the iniquities indulged before the seat of jealousy, was this worshiping of the sun toward the east.

"O son of man . . . see greater abominations than these" (8:15, 16). Three months before the declaration of war in 1914 a great sun festival was held in Paris. Selah.

Sun dances were the order of the day and hymns were sung to the sun. It is a wonder of wonders that a holy God endures such insults to His sacred majesty and government. Such abominations deserve the swift judgments of an offended Deity. The full and final defeat of France is inevitable. The destruction of such God-forsaking nations and individuals must be a persistent demand of the angels of God.

8

THE MAN WITH THE WRITER'S INKHORN

EZEKIEL 9

SCRIPTURE	EXPOSITION
"Behold, six men"	God's destroying angels, ministers of wrath. Two were sent against Sodom, six were sent against Jerusalem.
"a slaughter weapon in his hand"	Day of mercy past, each angelic minister of vengeance is prepared for his work.
"and one man"	The Man Christ Jesus.
"was clothed with linen"	Priestly attire.
"with a writer's inkhorn by his side"	As a recording clerk of court. Christ is here as the righteous Mediator and Judge. Those written in the Lamb's book of life will be saved.
"and they went in"	The six warrior angels.
"and stood"	Waiting for orders.
"beside the brasen altar"	At this altar sin was judged, and upon this altar the sacrificial victim died. No lamb, heifer or bullock, and no blood is here mentioned and hence no atonement.
"the glory of God . . . was gone"	Persistent sin means the departure of God. God was about to leave the temple. His glory was already departing.

"to the threshhold" — God departing but desiring to stay. God is loath to leave His people.

"Go . . . and set a mark" — Satan and Antichrist mark their followers. Sin marks its devotees and God marks His own sheep.

"upon . . . the men that sigh and that cry" — Those separated from the sin of the city were to be saved. *Sighing* inwardly and *crying* outwardly so as to warn others, these intercessors were to be spared, they were marked. As the blood upon the doorposts of Egypt so the mark on the foreheads of the separated and praying few. If we will keep clean and pure, God will keep us safe and secure.

"and to the others" — The other five angels.

"he said, Go" — They stood at attention, ready for orders and now the order is given, GO. Judgment begins at the house of God and among the people of God.

"Go ye after him" — Follow the man with the inkhorn setting a mark upon the saints who are separated from the sins of the city and temple.

"through the city" — Jerusalem—every house!

"and smite" — The Dove of mercy having fled, their cup of iniquity filled to overflowing *"smite"* let not your eye spare, neither have you pity";

"and begin at my sanctuary"

Judgment always begins at the house of God. How dreadful to think that a person may go to hell from a church choir and drop into perdition from the sacred pulpit.

Begin at the temple. Begin in Jerusalem. Begin the slaughter among the children of Israel, the people of God.

"Then they began at the ancient men"

The elders of Israel were the first to feel the judgment stroke. The first to be smitten were the preachers, e l d e r s, those who should have been warning watchmen. The hottest hell will be the hell of faithless preachers and teachers.

"and he said unto them. Defile the house and fill the courts with the slain"

Filled with fear, many would run to the altar and lay hold upon the altar but an altar without sprinkled blood upon it, cannot save. These people and priests alike would perish in the temple and at the altar and thus the house be defiled, and the courts be filled with the dead and dying. The love of God is wonderful, "and they went forth and slew in the city"

the wrath of God is awful. The wheat was first gathered and garnered and then the chaff burned and destroyed.

The wages of sin is death.

"and it came to pass while they were slaying . . . and I was left"

A thousand fell at his right hand and a thousand more at his left hand but the destruction did not come nigh Ezekiel. Purity and separation means protection and safety.

Holiness means heaven though hell is all around.

"I fell upon my face, and cried, and said, Ah, Lord God!"

The patience of God was exhausted. His love had been so spurned, His grace so despised, and His will so disregarded that prayer was unavailing. How dreadful to grieve the Spirit until God departs and departs for ever.

"Then said he unto me, The iniquity of the house of Israel and Judah is exceedingly great, and the land is full of blood, and the city full of perverseness: for they say, *The Lord* hath forsaken the earth, and the Lord *seeth not*. And as for me also mine eye shall not spare, neither will I have pity, but I will recompense their way upon their head."

9

THE SIGN OF EZEKIEL'S REMOVING

EZEKIEL 12-13

"The word of the Lord also came unto me, saying, Son of man, thou dwellest in the midst of a rebellious house, which have *eyes to see, and see not; they have ears to hear, and hear not: for they are a rebellious house.* Therefore, thou son of man, prepare thee stuff for removing, and remove by day in their sight; and thou shalt remove from thy place to another place in their sight: it may be they will consider, though they be a rebellious house. Then shalt thou bring forth thy stuff by day in their sight, as stuff for removing: and thou shalt go forth at even in their sight, as they that go forth into captivity. Dig thou through the wall in their sight, and carry out thereby."

SCRIPTURE	EXPOSITION
"Therefore,"	The people had eyes but were blind. They had ears but were deaf. They were in darkness because of sin and stubbornness, *therefore,* show them by signs, symbols, actions, and riddles. "Therefore, thou son of man."
"prepare thee stuff for removing"	Thus is pictured the coming captivity. Prepare for a journey. Get ready to

travel. "Prepare thee stuff for removing.

"Dig thou through the wall"

These action pictures must have astonished the onlookers. As a prisoner seeking to escape, Ezekiel was to smash his way through a wall. The gates of the city closed and locked, Ezekiel was to attempt an escape by digging through the wall.

"and carry out thereby"

Take your furniture through the hole you have digged in the wall. What a tiresome, laborious and impossible task.

"thou shalt cover thy face"

Ashamed and afraid.

"that thou see not the ground"

Eyes, but blinded.

"I have set thee for a sign"

Warning and working, preaching and teaching by example.

"And I did so as I was commanded"

He obeyed implicitly every command. He did all he could for the good of others. He was willing to be ridiculous and do ridiculous things to help save his brethren. He was ready to move out at a moment's notice. Neither home, wife nor friends hindered him in the walk and way of holiness and duty. What a picture! A holy man digging through a wall *with his hand,* carrying his goods upon his own shoulder and early in the morning, crawling through the hole with a covering over his face. Selah!

Yet shall he not see it (12:13).

Zedekiah was warned by Jeremiah but refused to heed the warning. Captured by Nebuchadnezzar and taken captive to Babylon, Zedekiah's eyes were put out by the cruel king before arriving in Babylon. Instead of becoming their savior as the people so foolishly hoped and believed, Zedekiah the prince was captured, his eyes put out, and plunged into hopeless darkness, he was carried to Babylon where he died.

They shall know that I am the Lord (12:15).

The scattered, dispersed, distressed and downtrodden Jews are living witnesses of their own sin and shame, and, also down to the minute witnesses of the truthfulness of God's Word.

Times that are far off (12:27).

The wickedness, waywardness, wilfulness and haughtiness of the human heart is unchanged. Ezekiel warned of impending judgment and doom. The people replied, "The vision . . . is for many days to come."

Ezekiel prophesied of imminent vengeance and wrath and the people replied, "He prophesieth of the times that are far off." What impudence and unbelief. What recklessness and rebellion. Even while they thus argued, the glory of the Lord had already departed and doom was at the door. It is just the same today. Earnest souls, in both pulpit and pew, urge God's people to holiness of heart and life in view of the near coming of the Lord, and the reply comes back to them as of yore, "My Lord delayeth his coming."

"Therefore say unto them, Thus saith the Lord God; There shall none of my words be prolonged any more, but the word which I have spoken shall be done."

Say unto them which daub it with untempered mortar (13:11).

Ezekiel, chapter thirteen, gives a concise definition of a false prophet, preacher and teacher.

1. He speaks out of his own heart (v. 2).

2. He utters his own mind (v. 3).

3. He disregards the Word of God (v. 3).

4. He is sly, and cunning (v. 4).

5. He is a devourer and wrecker (v. 5).

6. He is self-called and self-commissioned (v. 6).

7. He cries peace when there is no peace (v. 10).

8. He whitewashes the people (v. 11).

9. He scoffs at the judgments of God (v. 22).

10. He strengthens the hands of the wicked by promising life (v. 22).

Here is a perfect picture of Russellism, Seventh Day Adventism, Spiritism, Christian Science, Theosophy, M o r m o n i s m and all the no-hellisms strengthening the hands of the wicked by promising life when God has plainly declared, "The wages of sin is death."

Woe to the women that sew pillows to all armholes (13:18).

The prophet here rebukes the foolish and unfaithful daughters of Zion who sat at ease and rested in supposed comfort and safety notwithstanding the warnings and rumblings of approaching doom. Their mysticism and occultism, like modern spiritism, and theosophy together with so-called Christian Science, were obnoxious to a holy God. Judgment, death and doom were certain.

Instead of rest and repose there would be wreck and ruin (v. 20). Their mysticism and occultism would end in the massacre of men and maids for the storm was about to break upon their unholy heads.

Woe to the women (13:18).

Spiritism, Christian Science, Theosophy and Pillar of Fire-ism are all woman made and woman inspired religions. They all set forth an easy, restful, armchair, flowery-bed-of-ease way to get to heaven. Sowing pillows to armholes (ease) and making kerchiefs upon the head (mysticism and occultism) are all attempts to climb up some other way.

Strengthened the hands of the wicked (13:22).

Russellism and Rutherfordism and all other no-hellites, strengthen the hands of the wicked by promising a second chance, or a second probation.

All holiness fighters make the heart of the righteous sad, and all who deny the existence of an everlasting hell for everlasting sinners strengthen the hands of the wicked, that he should not turn from his wicked way. If there is no hell, then there is no heaven and no God and there ought not to be any pest houses, penitentiaries, asylums, hospitals, or jails.

Promising life to the wicked (13:22).

Present day Rutherfordism with its so-called Jehovah's Witnesses, like Russellism of the past, makes the heart of the righteous sad by promising life to the wicked.

Neither the McQuilkins of Chicago, the Pilkingtons of Philadelphia nor the Russellites, Rutherfordites, nor any other hot-brained no-hellites can change the sentence, "The *soul* that sinneth it shall die." To assure criminals that there is no jail and no penitentiary strengthens the hands of the wicked here, and to assure sinners that there is no future punishment for sin in a future penitentiary somewhere, is certainly strengthening the hands of the wicked. If there is no hell then there is no heaven for no one deserves heaven.

As certain as heaven is at the end of the road for the believing and faithful, so hell is at the end of the highway of sin and unholiness. Russellism, Rutherfordism, Seventh Day Adventism and all the other no-hell doctrines were born in perdition, inspired by Satan and make the heart of the righteous sad by promising life, peace and no future punishment for sin to the wicked.

10

CROSSING THE DEADLINE

Ezekiel 14-15

12 The word of the Lord came again to me, saying,

13 Son of man, when the land sinneth against me by trespassing grievously, then will I stretch out mine hand upon it, and will break the staff of the bread thereof, and will send famine upon it, and will cut off man and beast from it:

14 Though these three men, Noah, Daniel, and Job, were in it, they should deliver but their own souls by their righteousness, saith the Lord God.

15 If I cause noisome beasts to pass through the land, and they spoil it, so that it be desolate, that no man may pass through because of the beasts:

16 Though these three men were in it, as I live, saith the Lord God, they shall deliver neither sons nor daughters, but the land shall be desolate.

17 Or if I bring a sword upon that land, and say, Sword, go through the land; so that I cut off man and beast from it:

18 Though these three men were in it, as I live, saith the Lord God, they shall deliver neither sons nor daughters, but they only shall be delivered themselves.

19 Or if I send a pestilence into that land, and pour out my fury upon it in blood, to cut off from it man and beast:

20 Though Noah, Daniel, and Job, were in it, as I live, saith the Lord God, they shall deliver neither son nor daughter; they shall but deliver their own souls by their righteousness.

(Ezekiel 14: 12-20)

God spared the cities of the plain because of the prayers and sanctity of Abraham. The house of Potiphar was blessed and prospered for the sake of the sanctified and prevailing Joseph.

The meditation and intercession of Moses shielded the people of God from judgment well deserved.

The ship in which Paul journeyed as well as all on board escaped destruction for the sake of Paul.

The prediluvian race was saved from utter extinction because of the righteous Noah.

Over and over again Daniel had prevailed with God and even Babylon was blessed and prosperous.

The perfection, purity and patience of Job are emphasized in both Testaments but *now* neither Noah, Daniel nor Job individually nor collectively can possibly keep back the oncoming judgments of Jehovah. The day of prevailing prayer with all its possibilities is passed.

Four times in Ezekiel fourteen it is definitely declared that though Noah, Daniel and Job were actually present, they should deliver but their own souls by their righteousness.

Thank God they would be saved, for God does not drown the righteous with the wicked. He does not burn up the believer when He pours forth His fury upon the brimstone swept cities of the plain.

The houses upon which blood has been sprinkled are always spared by the destroying angels. It is always safe to hide under the feathers of our heavenly Father and trust His eternal wings.

A thousand may fall around the believer, but the arrow falls beside him, it does not strike him down.

The Noah's of all ages who walk with God will find grace and an ark.

The greatly beloved Daniel's will always be saved from the great destructions.

The justified and sanctified Job's shall always be brought out with twice as much blessing as before the trial.

This city and people however had gone so far in shame and sin that while Noah, Daniel and Job would be saved, their influence and prayers now could save no one else.

When once the dead line is crossed intercession and influence of even sanctified saints is too late.

How tragic! How terrible! that a person, a city and a nation can cross the deadline beyond which there is no return and no redemption.

The Parable of the Vine (15: 1-7).

"And the word of the Lord came unto me, saying, Son of man, What is the vine tree more than
any tree, or than a branch which is among the trees
of the forest? Shall wood be taken thereof to do
any work? or will men take a pin of it to hang any
vessel thereon? Behold, it is cast into the fire for
fuel: the fire devoureth both the ends of it, and the
midst of it is burned. Is it meet for any work? Behold, when it was whole it was meet for no work;
how much less shall it be meet yet for any work,
when the fire hath devoured it, and it is burned?
Therefore thus saith the Lord God, As the vine tree
among the trees of the forest, which I have given to
the fire for fuel, so will I give the inhabitants of Jerusalem. And I will set my face against them; they
shall go out from one fire, and another fire shall de-
vour them; and ye shall know that I am the Lord,
when I set my face against them."

As the vine tree among the trees (15: 6).

A vineyard is for the purpose of obtaining grapes
and wine is intended to make glad the heart of God
and man. A vine tree without grapes is a cumberer
of the ground. It is worse than useless. Not only is
it fruitless itself, but it occupies space which may
be occupied by a *fruitful* tree. Without fruit the
vine tree is without value. Other trees are good
for shelter and fuel, but not so the vine tree. The
nation of Israel had become unfruitful and hence
unprofitable to God or man. Instead of producing

luscious grapes of Eshcol, it was a cumberer of the ground.

"Being then made free from sin . . .

"Ye have your fruit unto holiness . . .

"And the end everlasting life."

Without *the fruit* (holiness) all is in vain (Heb. 12: 14). God has no ultimate use for an unholy person. When the vine fails to produce grapes it fails altogether. It is grapes or nothing. Other trees are good for fuel but the vine is good for nothing if it fails to bear fruit. Other trees may be used for fences, tables and chairs, but if the vine fails to bear grapes it fails completely, totally, irremediably and absolutely.

It is simply impossible to get a peg out of the vine upon which to hang anything that is of the least weight. It is useful only for grapes and for grapes only. There is no middle ground. It is grapes or death. It is grapes or destruction. It is grapes or burning. It is grapes or fire. It is the same with the people of God.

11

THE SIGN OF THE ABANDONED CHILD

Ezekiel 16

Scripture	Exposition
"Thy birth and thy nativity is . . . Canaan"	The original inhabitants of Canaan were the descendants of Ham and were cursed (Gen. 9:25). Born in sin and shapen in iniquity.
"thy father was an Amorite"	As early in history as the days of Abraham, the Amorites were filling up the cup of their iniquity (Gen. 15:16).
"thy mother an Hittite"	Wicked, depraved and unclean enemies of God and Israel.
"None eye pitied thee"	Helpless, filthy, lost and undone.
"thou wast cast out in the open field"	The field is the world. Cast out—unwelcome, unwanted and unloved—to perish in its own filth and uncleanness.
"and when I passed by thee and saw thee"	Jehovah saw Satan on top, and the abandoned, helpless and hopeless child trodden under foot—about to perish. Thank God *He saw.*
"I said unto thee, *Live*"	"Ye must be born again."
"I have caused thee to multiply"	Born again and *fruitful.* The margin reads, "I have made

thee a million." A million—from one who was lost, helpless and hopeless.

Every child of God is a multiplication entity.

"thou hast increased and waxen great"

Growth, increase and multiplication is God's order. This was especially true of God's ancient people.

"thou art come to excellent ornaments"

Beauty and comeliness.

"thy breasts are fashioned"

Fully grown and developed and with nourishment, sustenance and support for others. A n d r e w found Peter. Philip found Nathanael.

"thine hair is grown"

Long hair is given to womankind for beauty and for covering. Woman's hair is her glory and the sign of her submission to God and angels. So-called bobbed haired beauties are backslidden.

"thy time was the time of love"

But no one loved and no one pitied.

"I spread my skirt over thee"

Covered by her Savior and Redeemer. Saved from perishing she was now covered with His robe.

"I entered into a covenant with thee"

Adoption.

"and thou becamest mine"

Mine by creation, *mine* by redemption, *mine* by protection, *mine* by adoption, and *mine* by regeneration.

"Then washed I thee with water"

The water of the Word, cleaning up the outside— the outward life. Regeneration fixes up the outward life.

"and I anointed thee with oil"

Sanctified wholly. Filled with the Spirit.

"I clothed thee — w i t h broidered work"

Hand work—service.

"and shod thee with badgers' skin"

Walk and not faint.

"I girded thee about with fine linen"

Holy and useful. "Fruitful in every good work." The life is to be clean and the hands are to be busy.

"I covered thee with silk"

Silk is obtained from a silkworm. The worm must die to provide this covering. Christ died that we might be kept covered with the silk of His own providing. Our own fig leaves cannot keep us covered. "I covered thy nakedness" (v. 8).

"I covered thee"

"I clothed thee (v. 10). "I covered thee" (v. 10). Nudism is of the devil.

"I decked thee also with ornaments"

The body belongs to the one who saved from perishing. "Your bodies are the temple of the Holy Ghost."

"I put bracelets upon thy hands"

Hands belong to Christ. Be careful how you use them. They are marked by the Savior.

"and a chain on thy neck"

The beauty of holiness—the proof that we belong to another—we are no longer our own.

"I put a jewel on thy forehead"

The head and face—including eyes, nose, lips and mouth—are marked for God and holiness. We are to think for God—watch and pray.

"and earrings in thine ears"

The ears belong to God— be careful about listening to gossip, slander — keep your eyes, lips and ears clean, *they are marked.* They belong to another, even Christ.

"and a beautiful crown upon thy head"

Royal and regal as well as redeemed. Battles fought, v i c t o r i e s won, crowns gained. Sure I must fight if I would win, increase my courage, Lord.

"thou didst eat fine flour, and honey, and oil"

Not leeks, onions, garlic and cucumbers, (food of Egypt —the world) not even manna which is wilderness food, but fine flour, honey and oil—holiness diet.

"thou wast exceeding beautiful"

Rescued from perishing, redeemed, r e g e n e r a t e d, washed, clothed, sanctified wholly, royal, regal and feasting on honey and fine flour, "Thou wast exceeding beautiful," in the sight of the one who rescued and redeemed.

"and thou didst prosper into a kingdom"

1. All this of course refers to Israel in the flesh—the kingdom under Saul, David and Solomon but
2. It also refers to Israel in the Spirit—the true Israel of God, the spiritual children of Abraham, the Church, a holy nation, a royal priesthood, a peculiar people.
3. It shall yet be perfectly fulfilled in the Millennial Kingdom of Christ.

"and thy renown went forth among the heathen"

The evangelization of the world. After conversion, regeneration and sanctification *then* comes evangelization. This is the divine order: (1) Come; (2) Tarry; (3) *Go*. Missions at home and abroad. Here is justification, followed by sanctification, followed by missionarification.

"for thy beauty"

The beauty of holiness— the work of evangelization will cause others to know the power and presence of God.

"for it was perfect"

Nothing less than perfection can satisfy God. Nothing short of this standard can satisfy the Redeemer.

	Perfection is God's standard.
	1. Perfection of heart now —perfection of love here in this life. "Be ye therefore perfect." "Let us therefore as many as be perfect, be thus minded." "Finally, brethren farewell, be perfect."
	2. Perfection of body and brain in the resurrection.
"through my comeliness"	All perfection, all goodness, all holiness is *through His* comeliness.
"which I had put upon thee."	All holiness, righteousness, goodness and perfection in the saints is imparted by Christ.

What a glowing picture—parable of full salvation, from the hog-pen to holiness, from slime to salvation, from filth to fullness, from ruin to redemption, from cursing to comeliness, from hell to heaven.

But (16:15).

One of the most glowing pictures of redemption from ruin, and salvation from sin ever penned, painted or portrayed is found in Ezekiel 16. Had the story ended at verse 14 all would have been serene and satisfying but so long as man is man, and sin is sin, and Satan is Satan and Christ is absent and evil is on the throne and holiness is on the scaffold, we may expect a *but* after the work of beauty, perfection, comeliness and holiness. Earth's

Edens do not last for long. Beauty soon turns to badness, perfection soon becomes putrefaction, comeliness soon is cursed and paradise becomes purgatory.

Israel had been loved, lured, lifted and honored above all peoples on the face of the earth. Rescued and redeemed, justified and sanctified, cleansed and purified, feasted and fattened, perfected and prosperous, *but*. But, flirting with the world—pandering to the flesh—deceived by the devil, and becoming lukewarm and lazy (how weak is thine heart).

God Almighty departed from them and they pined away in captivity. The Holy Ghost, who had led them, lifted His white wings and left them forever. Read the whole chapter.

12

THE RIDDLE OF THE TWO EAGLES

SCRIPTURE	EXPOSITION
"Son of man"	Ezekiel the prophet was linked to the whole human race. Not only was he a son of Abraham, Isaac and Jacob but like Christ he was a son of man. Nobler than all nationalities, Ezekiel was related to the race.
"put forth a riddle"	An obscure description of something in order to arouse the drowsy mind of the hearers.
"a great eagle"	Nebuchadnezzar. (See "Diamonds from Daniel.")
"with great wings"	Powerful and prosperous.
"longwinged"	Vast dominions — worldwide empire.
"full of feathers"	Subjects—peoples.
"which had divers colors"	Many nations.
"came unto Lebanon"	The royal house of David.
"and took the highest branch of the cedar"	The king.
"he cropped off the top of his young twigs"	1. Twigs i.e., the princes. 2. The top i.e., Jehoiakim.
"and carried it"	Captivity of Jehoiakim.
"into a land of traffick"	Assyria.
"he set it in a city of merchants"	Babylon.

"he took also of the seed of the land"	Zedekiah.
"and planted it in a fruitful field"	Jerusalem.
"he placed it beside great waters"	Provision for life, growth and development.
"and set it as a willow tree"	Growing quickly and very useful, but not intended to be great or stately.
"it grew and became a spreading vine"	Fruitful and useful.
"whose branches turned toward him"	The people looked toward Nebuchadnezzar.
"and the roots thereof were under him"	Dependent upon Nebuchadnezzar.
"so it became a vine"	Fulfilled the purpose for which it was planted.
"There was also another great eagle"	The king of Egypt.
"with great wings"	Powerful.
"and many feathers"	People.
"and, behold, this vine did bend her roots toward him"	Treachery—faithlessness—leaning toward the king of Egypt instead of being subject to Nebuchadnezzar.
"and shot forth her branches toward him"	Rebellion against Nebuchadnezzar and seeking help from Egypt.
"it was planted in a good soil"	Zedekiah's wonderful opportunity in Jerusalem.
"by great waters"	Plentiful provision under Nebuchadnezzar.
"that it might bring forth branches"	Growth and development of the nation of Israel.
"that it might bear fruit"	Fruitfulness and usefulness.
"that it might be a goodly vine "	Fulfilling the purposes for which it was planted, bring-

"Say thou, Thus saith the Lord God; Shall it prosper?"

ing gladness to God and man.
Shall Zedekiah's move for independence p r o s p e r? Shall treachery triumph? Shall Zedekiah prosper in his rebellion against Nebuchadnezzar?

"Shall he"

Nebuchadnezzar.

"not pull up the roots thereof"

Zedekiah.

"and cut off the fruit thereof"

The people.

"shall it not utterly wither, when the east wind toucheth it?"

With little trouble and effort Nebuchadnezzar shall put an end to the rebellion, defeat and destroy both the prince (Zedekiah) and the people (the house of Israel).

A "riddle" is intended to interest and excite the imagination. A good and gracious God seeks to arrest the attention of men in order to keep them out of hell and prepare them for heaven. If the gentle zephyr fails He sends the thunder. If the small silvery streamlet is silent, He sends the devastating storm. If the birth of a beautiful babe fails to bring us to our knees in thankfulness and gratitude then perhaps the funeral dirge and empty chair will accomplish our redemption. If the stars and flowers fail perhaps the storm and funeral will succeed.

13

THE CONQUERING KING OF BABYLON

(Ezekiel 17:11-21)

SCRIPTURE	EXPOSITION
"Behold, the king of Babylon"	Nebuchadnezzar
"is come to Jerusalem"	The capital city of David and the house of Israel.
"and hath taken the king thereof and the princes thereof"	The royal house of David.
"and led them with him to Babylon"	The captivity.
"and hath taken of the king's seed"	Zedekiah.
"and made a covenant with him"	An agreement.
"and hath taken an oath of him"	Nebuchadnezzar took Mattaniah (youngest son of Josiah) and changed his name to Zedekiah. Zedekiah made an agreement, an oath with Nebuchadnezzar.
"he"	Nebuchadnezzar.
"hath also taken the mighty of the land";	The leaders—chief men.
"that the kingdom"	Israel.
"might be base"	Kept in subjection under Nebuchadnezzar.

"but that by keeping of his covenant it might stand."

The kingdom of Israel and Judah would stand if the agreement was kept by Zedekiah the prince or governor under Nebuchadnezzar.

"But he rebelled"

Zedekiah went back on his word and oath.

"against him"

Zedekiah rebelled against Nebuchadnezzar.

"Shall he prosper?"

Shall Zedekiah succeed?

"shall he break the covenant and be delivered?"

Shall Zedekiah go back on his word and oath and be delivered by the help of Egypt?

"As I live, saith the Lord God, surely"

No question as to the consequences.

"in the place where the king dwelleth"

1. The place (Babylon)
2. The king (Nebuchadnezzar).

"that made him king"

Zedekiah was made king by Nebuchadnezzar.

"whose oath he despised"

Zedekiah had sworn allegiance to Nebuchadnezzar.

"he shall die"

Zedekiah's death sentence. Zedekiah was taken according to the word of the Lord. His eyes were put out, his sons were slain, and he died a prisoner in Babylon.

The Word of God is sure against both wilful sinners and wayward saints.

14

THE PARABLE OF THE HIGH CEDAR

(Ezekiel 17:22-24)

Scripture	Exposition
"Thus saith the Lord God, I will also take of the highest branch of the high cedar"	The Royal House of David.
"I will crop off . . . a tender one and will plant it upon an high mountain"	Christ
"it shall bring forth boughs and bear fruit"	People. Fruitful people.
"and be a goodly cedar"	Profitable and prosperous.
"and under it shall dwell all fowl"	Protection and provision. Picture of the Millennial Kingdom of Christ.
"and all the trees of the field shall know"	Gentile world powers.
"I have brought down the high tree"	Assyria.
"Have exalted the low tree"	Judah.
"have dried up the green tree"	Babylon.
"And made the dry tree to flourish"	Israel.

The high tree was Assyria under Nebuchadnezzar, while the low tree was Judah, made low by the judgments of God, consequent upon their sin, lust and lawlessness.

The green tree, great and flourishing, was Babylon under the mighty power of the first world monarch, while the dry tree was Israel, made dry and destitute because of their disobedience to God. God Almighty here winds up the riddle, the parable, the story in His own inimitable way. He sets forth the purpose of all His strange dealings and providences by saying, "And all the trees of the field shall know that I the Lord have brought down the high, . . . have exalted the low, . . . have dried up the green, . . . and have made the dry, . . . to flourish." This is true to all human life. God is the Governor and Guardian of all the universe. The last word is His.

The children's teeth are set on edge (18: 2).

The wilful, wayward, sinful and stubborn Israelites used a proverb saying, "The fathers have eaten sour grapes, and the children's teeth are set on edge," insinuating that they were being punished for their fathers' sins, and not for their own! *The proverb is not true* and ought not to be used by Christians. It is not true for the following reasons:

1. Some fathers are good and their children are evil.

2. Some fathers are evil and their sons are good.

3. Some fathers are strong and their sons are weaklings.

4. Some fathers are weak and their sons are strong.

5. Some fathers are devils and their sons are fire-baptized holiness preachers.

6. Some fathers are preachers and their sons are in the penitentiary. Josiah was the pious and pure son of a wicked father.

7. Whether father or son, "the soul that sinneth it shall die," but if a man be just and do that which is right in the sight of God, whether father or son, "he shall surely live."

If the sins of the fathers come upon the children as a punishment by God it is because the children follow the fathers' wicked ways.

Why will ye die? (18:31).

"Therefore I will judge you, O house of Israel, every one according to his ways, saith the Lord God. Repent, and turn yourselves from all your transgressions; so iniquity shall not be your ruin.

Cast away from you all your transgressions, whereby ye have transgressed, and make you a new heart and a new spirit; for why will ye die, O house of Israel?

For I have no pleasure in the death of him that dieth, saith the Lord God; wherefore turn yourselves, and live ye."

This eighteenth chapter of Ezekiel for the second time levels a sledge hammer blow to the theory of "eternal sonship" or "once in grace always in grace."

Verse 24, "But when the righteous turneth away from his righteousness, and committeth iniquity, and doeth according to all the abominations that the wicked man doeth, shall he live? All his righteousness that he hath done shall not be mentioned: in his trespass that he hath trespassed, and in his sin that he hath sinned, in them shall he die." There can be no appeal from this scripture of truth. Arguments are useless. Debate is impossible. God has spoken.

"Again when a righteous man doth turn away from his righteousness, and commit iniquity, and I lay a stumblingblock before him, he shall die: because thou hast not given him warning, he shall die in his sin, and his righteousness which he hath done shall not be remembered; but his blood will I require at thy hand."

15

LIONS, THE LIONESS AND HER WHELPS

EZEKIEL 19

SCRIPTURE	EXPOSITION
"Take . . . up a lamentation"	This is a lamentation of Jehovah. This is God's wail, God's cry, God's sorrow.
"for the princes of Israel"	1. Jehoahaz—taken to Egypt. 2. Jehoiachin—to Babylon.
"and say, What is thy mother?"	Judah.
"A lioness: she lay down"	At ease and enjoying rest in the days of Solomon, despite powerful nations around.
"among lions"	Nations and kings of the earth.
"she nourished her whelps"	Sons of the house of David.
"among young lions"	Nations.
"and she brought up one of her whelps"	One of her sons.
"it became a young lion"	King.
"and it learned to catch the prey"	Victorious.
"it devoured men"	Jehoahaz did evil in the sight of the Lord.
"the nations also heard of him"	Gentile nations round about him.
"he was taken in their pit"	Captured.

"and they brought him with chains"	Bound and imprisoned.
"unto the land of Egypt"	Captivity in Egypt.
"She took another of her whelps"	Another son.
"and made him a young lion"	King Jehoiachin.
"and he went up and down among the lions"	Nations.
"he learned to catch the prey"	Cunning and victorious.
"and devoured men"	Did evil in the sight of the Lord.
"and the land was desolate"	Exploitations and wars.
"then the nations set against him"	The Gentile nations.
"he was taken in their pit"	Captured and imprisoned.
"and brought him to the king of Babylon"	Jehoiachin was taken captive to Babylon. Sin spells slavery. Disobedience means death.

16

THE RIDDLE OF THE VINE AND STRONG RODS

EZEKIEL 19:10

SCRIPTURE	EXPOSITION
"Thy mother"	Judah.
"is like a vine"	Fruitful.
"planted by the waters"	Provision and preservation.
"she was fruitful and full of branches"	Sons and people.
"and she had strong rods"	(1) David. (2) Solomon. (3) Jehoahaz. (4) Jehoiachin. (5) Jehoiakim.
"But she was plucked up in fury"	By Nebuchadnezzar.
"the east wind"	The Chaldeans.
"dried up her fruit"	Usefulness and fruitfulness destroyed.
"her strong rods were broken"	Jehoahaz, Jehoiachin and Jehoiakim.
"and now she is planted in the wilderness, in a dry and thirsty ground"	Egypt and Babylon.
"and fire is gone out of a rod of her branches"	Zedekiah's foolishness and treachery.
"so that she hath no strong rod, to rule."	No king. True to this very hour.

Sin is the most destructive, the most devastating, the most costly thing in all the universe of God.

It swept into captivity and sorrow the last remnant of God's Chosen People. It does not pay to tinker with conscience or trifle with the truth of God. Sin ends in sighing and slavery, darkness and death.

17

THE SABBATH QUESTION SETTLED FOREVER

EZEKIEL 20-22

My sabbath . . . a sign (20:12).

"My sabbaths . . . a sign . . . sanctify them"

"Moreover also I gave them my sabbaths, to be a sign between me and them, that they might know that I am the Lord that doth sanctify them" (20: 12).

Here is the answer to the oft-repeated question, "Why the Sabbath?" (1) Rest after work. God rested. (2) Man's temporal and eternal benefit. (3) God's ownership of our time. One tree in the garden of Eden, one-seventh of our time and one-tenth of all our income—claimed by God. (4) Our entire sanctification. The issue therefore is *not* Saturday or Sunday but sanctification. The big thing is *entire sanctification and soul rest.* It matters little, if anything at all, what day of the week we keep holy unless the heart is made holy. A holy heart issuing in a holy life will keep each day and every day holy and the first day of the week which commemorates the resurrection of our Lord Jesus Christ will become a peculiarly sacred and holy day in which to worship God and work with might for the salvation of others.

Ah Lord God! . . . Doth he not speak parables? (20: 49).

By signs, riddles, parables, pictures, actions, types and symbols, God Almighty sought to get the truth home to the stubborn hearts and stuffed ears of His people, but all in vain.

The prophet in these four closing verses sees the wrath of God sweeping the cities of Judah like a forest fire, "the flaming flame," burning all faces from the south to the north. How dreadful to bring down on one's own head the devastating fire and fury of an outraged Deity.

The Sign of the Sigh (21:1-7).

Ezekiel twenty-one sets forth (1) The impending judgments upon Jerusalem (1-24). (2) The promise of Christ whose right it is to reign (25-27), and (3) The ruin of the Ammonites (28-32).

Verses one to seven sets forth the sign of the sighing prophet, while verses 8-17 sets forth the Sign of the Sword.

Sin ends in sighing and swords. Sin is the most expensive thing in the universe of God. It is the most destructive thing in our world today. There is nothing so hard to slay as sin. A gnat or a pebble may pulverize a giant; a word may break the peace of the world; a spark may burn up a city; but who can destroy the monster in the heart of man, the serpent of sin.

Every sigh and cry of every mother and babe is the direct or indirect result of sin.

Sin is a deceiving Delilah that destroys and damns.

Sin tickles while it stabs and then later torments the soul. Sin bewitches and then puts out the eyes.

Sin smites under the fifth rib as Joab smote Abner. It is a dragon that destroys, a serpent that slays and a poison that pervades the whole man.

We must get rid of it or be damned.

Thou, profane wicked prince (21: 25).

Ezekiel twenty-one contains three main subjects:

1. The impending judgment upon Jerusalem (1-24).

2. The wicked prince and his *end* (25-27).

3. The awful doom of the Ammonites (28-32).

Nebuchadnezzar stood at the fork of the roads, at the parting of the ways, uncertain whether to attack the Ammonites or Judah. Praying to his gods, consulting his knives and teraphim, and gazing into the liver of a sheep as a gazer sits before the crystal ball, he pretends to receive the answer and starts on the road to Jerusalem as the rod and scourge of God against His backslidden people. It is a fearful thing to fall into the hands of the living God.

Zedekiah was the profane and wicked prince and a type of the coming Antichrist whose day shall come when iniquity shall have an end. Here is a prophecy of the return of Christ, whose right it is to reign (v. 27). Christ shall yet receive the diadem.

He shall yet be given the crown, and He shall reign forever.

The Sins of Saints

(A Catalog)

(22: 1-12)

Man sinks far lower than the beasts of the field. It is an insult to the animal world to compare some men to beasts. Man is capable of much more greed and lust than the hog, he is far more ferocious than the lion and more brutal than the bear. Buzzards and polecats are decent compared to some tobacco soaks and drunken bums in many of our streets and cities. Suffer the skunk but save me from the slaves of tobacco and strong drink. The awful wickedness, corruptions and abominations committed by Israel called for the just judgments of God.

Practices worthy of death, doom and damnation brought swift punishment upon the perpetrators. The threatened judgments fell and swept away the chosen nation.

Such profane, wretched, miserable and polluted people must perish in order that the race should survive and the plans of God be fulfilled.

To permit such impure people to survive would ruin and curse the whole human family, make impossible the Coming of Christ and add earth to the dominion of hell.

The king of Babylon prayed to his gods and at the fork of the roads consulted his idols, looked into the liver of a sheep (21:21) decided to attack Jerusalem, and Israel was taken with the hand (21:24).

Sin scorches the soul, blasts and blights the life and ends in the blackness of darkness forever.

I sought for a man . . . I found none (22:30).

To read this chapter of Ezekiel makes the blood turn to ice, and then boil with indignation. The wilful wickedness, the abominable corruptions committed by Israel undoubtedly deserve the death, doom and damnation of which they have been warned. It is distinctly an act of mercy toward the human race as a whole to devastate and destroy utterly, such profane, wicked, polluted people.

To permit such to live would forever curse the race of mankind and would slowly but surely result in earth becoming a pandemonium of gathering impurity fit only for perdition. It is an insult to the animal world, to say that man is like the beast of the field, for mankind sinks far lower than the beasts are capable of sinking. Israel had become defiled, polluted idolaters and adulterers, reasonless and senseless, filthy and heathenish. They had degenerated and had become devilutionized and demonized. They had become dross, brass, tin, iron and lead instead of gold, silver and precious jewels. Consequently they would be flung into a roaring furnace of fire until they felt the fury of an insulted and outraged God.

The leaders and teachers of the people had become lucre loving and lustful. They had violated

God's holy law, profaned God's holy things, and daubed the people with untempered mortar by preaching smooth things. They had vexed the poor and needy, oppressed the stranger, disregarded the difference between holy and unholy, and clean and unclean, until princes, teachers, preachers and people alike were calling down the vengeance of Jehovah. God sought for an Abraham to plead for these Sodomites but could not find him. Not one. God looked for a man that should make up the hedge, a Moses or an Aaron who would stand in the gap, but not one could be found. There was no intercessor, no mediator, no daysman, no Abraham, no Moses, no Aaron, no Joshua, no Paul, no John, no Luther, and no Wesley.

"Therefore have I poured out my indignation upon them; I have consumed them with the fire of my wrath; their own way have I recompensed upon their heads, saith the Lord God" (v. 31).

18

THE STORY OF TWO SISTERS

Ezekiel 23

Scripture	Exposition
"There were two women"	(1) Israel. (2) Judah.
"and they committed whoredoms in Egypt"	The line of separation broken down.
"in their youth"	Flirting and fooling with the world.
"and the names of them were Aholah"	Israel (Samaria)
"and Aholibah"	Judah (Jerusalem)
"And Aholah played the harlot when she was mine"	Israel belonged to God by creation, calling, redemption and preservation.
"and she doted on her lovers"	Forgetting the One true lover of her soul, she fell for the lovers of her body.
"wherefore I have delivered her into the hand of her lovers"	The Children of Israel were taken captive by the Assyrians.
"and when her sister Aholibah saw this"	Judah saw the punishment inflicted upon Israel *but* refused the warning and persisted in her evil way.
"I saw that she was defiled"	Disobedience spells defilement and pollution.
"that they took both one way"	Israel and Judah were both set on their own *evil* way.
"then my mind was alienated from her"	Judah had forsaken the Lord and now the Lord forsakes Judah.

"like as my mind was alienated from her sister." — Israel.

"And I will set my jealousy against thee" — The God of Abraham, Israel and Judah is a jealous God.

"and they shall deal furiously with thee" — The Babylonians and the Chaldeans. Judah.

"they shall take away thy nose and thine ears" — Cut off the nose. Cut off the ears, as Samson's eyes were put out, so the nose and ears of the Jews would be cut off.

"and they shall deal with thee hatefully" — Mutilations of face and body.

"thou shalt pluck off thine own breasts" — Mad with pain and insane with sorrow and suffering.

"thou paintedst thy eyes" — Like Hollywood movie stars, and even like *some professed Christians. Selah.*

"and deckedst thyself with ornaments" — Instead of a meek and quiet spirit. Better quit that crowd.

"and satest upon a stately bed" — Ease and pleasure.

"Thus saith the Lord, I will give them to be spoiled—their sons and daughters shall be slain and their houses burned with fire" — The Assyrian spoilers shall slay their children, destroy their homes and lead them captive.

"that all women may be taught." —

"Thus will I cause lewdness to cease out of the land; that all women may be taught not to do after your lewdness" (v. 48).

*The Perversities and Impurities of Preachers,
...Priests, Princes and People* (22: 23-31; 23: 1-49)

Running through mythology and art as well as Scripture, the dragon is history's first symbol of sin, and the serpent is the first symbol of Satan.

A snake winding his scaly length round and round the globe called earth has always represented the universality of sin.

Faithful preachers and people have always been the salt of the earth—unfaithful and hireling preachers together with hypocritical professors of all ages have always been a hindrance to the cause of God and holiness.

Sin, whether committed by sinner or saint, priest or people, is a fearful thing.

The First Sin committed is still running like currents of fire and rampaging floods through all the ramifications of our race.

The First Sin, one sin—has made the earth heave, sigh, surge and groan. It has robbed heaven of some of its symphonic stars. It has built the soundproof walls of an eternal prison, kindled its first and now unquenchable fires and given birth to the worm that never dies.

The groans of men, women and children, and animals, if gathered together would be sufficient to split the rocks asunder. The sighs and cries and tears of humans, if collected, would make a roaring Atlantic without a moment's calm.

Sin is the thing which God hates and which He has determined to destroy.

We must part with sin or sin will separate us from God forever.

"The Boiling Pot and Burning Bones" (24:1-14).

As a rope or cable is twined from many threads so sin becomes a coiling serpent which ends in burning and boiling. Boiling and burning are the end of all backsliding. Selah!

A gash in the head of a man may be healed but the scar remains. The scar will be seen in the casket.

Sinning against God, Christ and the Bible is also sinning against one's own soul and it always leaves a scar.

Neither repentance nor confessions nor coffins can rub out or hide the sin-scarred marks upon the soul of man.

Sin pollutes and poisons and nothing short of the fiery baptism with the Spirit of God can possibly rid the soul of the scorching, damning disease of sin. We must have sin burned out of us, cleansed out of us, or we must boil and burn in it.

This terrifying picture of a boiling pot and burning bones should make us afraid to sin against a holy God.

Sin is a departure from God and holiness. Any want of conformity to His Word or will is sin, and sin ends in judgment and death. Any transgression of the law of God is an unleashing of the forces of damnation. To commit any sin is consummate folly. To brag and boast about sin is diabolical and fiendish. Sin is a mass murder of the mind of the man. We must get rid of it or it will assuredly get rid of us. Sin must be destroyed or it will destroy the soul forever. Sin may promise life, pleasure and profit, but its wages is death, destruction and perdition. Anyone who will compare the promises of sin and the payments of sin will discover the deceits and falsehoods of both sin and Satan. As certain as God is God, sin ends in sorrow, suffering, shame, death and damnation, world without end. Its beginnings can be bright and light as the mornings but its end is the darkness of the blackest night.

The Sign of the Death of Ezekiel's Wife (24: 15-27).

"Son of man, behold, I take away from thee the desire of thine eyes with a stroke: yet neither shalt thou mourn nor weep, neither shall thy tears run down. Forbear to cry, make no mourning for the dead, bind the tire of thine head upon thee, and put on thy shoes upon thy feet, and cover not thy lips, and eat not the bread of men. So I spake unto the people in the morning; and at even my wife died: and I did in the morning as I was commanded. And the people said unto me, Wilt thou not tell us what these things are to us, that thou doest so?"

Ezekiel the prophet was a living, moving, talking, acting sign to the people of God. He had to bind himself, shut himself up in prison, lie upon his right side 390 days and then upon his left side 40 days, eat defiled and polluted bread, shave his head with a knife, and his face with a razor, and carry a captive's baggage through a hole digged in the wall by his own hand. As a fitting climax to the whole, his wife (the desire of his eyes) was to suddenly die, and the broken-hearted son of man was forbidden to cry. Relief through tears was denied him.

"Son of man, behold, I take away from thee the desire of thine eyes with a stroke; yet neither shalt thou mourn nor weep, neither shall thy tears run down."

Unquestioning obedience befits this son of man —type of our Lord Jesus Christ bearing the sin, shame, sorrow and reproach of His people.

God sets all His signs to the times. Ezekiel was a sign (1) because he willingly sacrificed all his personal and private interests to the glory of God; (2) because he was willing and ready to take any position or attitude to please God; (3) because he sacrificed the desire of his eyes and ran right across the course of this world.

The first law given by God to man was the law of obedience. From obedience and submission to God spring all other virtues. No principle is more sublime and none is more holy than that of unquestioning obedience to God. It is not ours to reason why, but ours to observe because it is commanded. True obedience does not ask questions and does not procrastinate. Prompt and implicit obedience to God and His Word is the only infallible proof of our sincere and supreme love to Him. It is the only highway to holiness, happiness and heaven.

Thou shalt be no more dumb (24: 27).

Stricken dumb by terror of the coming torments, the prophet would be delivered in due course and his speech return.

These horrible descriptions of awful tribulation to come upon the Jews look forward to the terrors of the Great Tribulation in the last days.

These pen pictures look beyond the immediate and imminent doom of Jerusalem in the days of Zedekiah to the closing scene of the Great Tribulation and the profane, wicked prince Antichrist of the last days.

PART THREE
Judgments Against the Gentiles

19

THE FATE OF TYRE AND OTHER FAITHLESS NATIONS

EZEKIEL 25-28

Outside of the prophecies of Isaiah in the Old Testament and the Apocalypse in the New Testament there is nothing to equal these chapters in any literature in any land. It is dangerous to live near some cities, some nations, some people and some institutions. Everything about the city of Tyre was beautiful but man, and he had become bestial, wicked and sinful. Consequently both he and the city were cursed. Where are all the wonderful cities of antiquity? What has become of all the pomp and pride and pleasure of Egypt, Tyre, Babylon, Greece and Persia. They sinned against God and were destroyed. ". . . Aha" (26:2). This one word, "Aha," took Tyrus over the deadline. This one cynical, simple sneer cost Tyrus her life. Tyrus was rebuked, stripped and humbled because she sneered at God's city and God's people. Sneering is spiritual suicide. The moment a man sneers at God or salvation that moment God begins preparing a storm that will soon break upon his sinful head. Sinners may sneer in the saloon or on the race course but sneering at God or the Bible or holiness or the Church or at the people of God invites sure and certain disaster and doom. "There-fore . . . behold, I am against thee, O Tyrus."

Chapters 25 to 32 set forth the judgments of God against the Gentiles.

1. The Ammonites.
2. The Moabites.
3. The Edomites.
4. The Philistines.
5. Tyre.
6. Sidon.
7. Egypt.

I shall bring up the deep upon thee (26:19).

Tyre, the once proud, pompous, prosperous and powerful city, the England of antiquity, was to be covered by the waters of the deep. So fully and completely have these prophecies been fulfilled, the critics have concluded that the record must have been written after the events. The exact site of Tyre cannot now be determined.

PERDITION . . . *With them that descend into the pit* (26:20).

A new section begins with chapter twenty-five. The following chapters contain predictions concerning seven Gentile nations in general, and all the Gentiles in particular. Complete fulfillment of these profound prophecies will be in the future. Ammon, Moab, Edom and the Philistines have each heard their doom pronounced and in chapter twenty-six and verse 20, Tyre, the glory of the Gentiles, is warned that the pit of perdition is just ahead.

"The people of old time," had been brought down to hell because of their sin and haughtiness, the people of Noah's day had brought upon themselves swift and irrevocable doom, the people of Sodom, "The people of old time" (26:20) had sinned away their day of grace and had been destroyed by fire and brimstone and had been swept into perdition's pit, and now Tyre was headed in the same direction and bound for the same fate. Sin and shame end in Sheol. Haughtiness and high-mindedness in Tyre or Sodom must end up in Hades. Hell is at the end of sin's highway. "I shall bring thee down with them that descend into the pit with the people of old time." "The people of old time" has reference to the Cainites who perished in the flood and the Sodomites who were devoured by the fires of a furious, sin-judging God.

20

THE ORIGIN OF EVIL

The anointed cherub that covereth (28:14).

A careful study of Ezekiel 28 and Isaiah 14 with Isaiah 45: 18, and Genesis 1: 2, reveals the following indisputable facts. Satan or the devil, sinful and wicked as he is, was created in beauty, wisdom, might and perfection. Before the creation of man he was anointed as ruler over the world. Snatching at equality with Christ he sinned against God and Lucifer became the monster of iniquity and the confirmed, unchanging, and unchangeable enemy of God. Resenting the creation of man and man's dominion over the earth, Satan planned his downfall and destruction. Through this satanic conquest and victory over man, Satan has regained in a measure his title of prince, ruler and god of this world.

Ten distinct titles are given Satan in the Scriptures; as the tempter, he is called the *devil*. Because of his cruelty he is described as the *great red dragon*. Since he is a master seducer he is called the *serpent*. Having become the adversary of God, he is named *Satan*. Being the head of the world's religion, he is the *god of this world*. He is also revealed as a roaring lion, an angel of light and the prince of the power of the air. He blinds the mind, accuses the brethren, sows tares among God's wheat and catches away the seed as it is sown. At the end of this present evil age he will incarnate himself in the oncoming man of sin, the Antichrist, and will compel the world to worship him. Saints are exhorted to "resist the devil" and refuse to give place to him.

I will destroy thee, O covering cherub (28:16).

These words certainly look beyond any ordinary man, king, prince or nation.

1. "I am of perfect beauty" (27:3).

2. "I am a God, I sit in the seat of God (28:2).

3. "Wiser than Daniel" (28:3).

4. "Thou hast set thine heart as the heart of God" (28:6).

5. "I am God" (28:9).

6. "Thou sealest up the sum, full of wisdom, and perfect in beauty" (28:12).

7. "Thou hast been in Eden, the garden of God" (28:13).

8. "The workmanship of thy tabrets and of thy pipes was prepared in thee in the day that thou wast *created*" (28:13).

9. "Thou art the anointed cherub that covereth; and I have set thee so" (28:14).

10. "Thou wast upon the holy mountain of God" (28:14).

11. "Thou hast walked up and down in the midst of the stones of fire" (28:14).

12. "Thou wast perfect in thy ways" (28:15).

13. "Perfect—from the day that thou wast *created*" (28:15).

14. "Thou wast perfect in thy ways from the day that thou wast created, till iniquity was found in thee" (28:15).

15. "Thou hast sinned; therefore I will cast thee as profane out of the mountain of God" (28:16).

16. "I will destroy thee, O covering cherub" (28:16).

17. "Thine heart was lifted up because of thy beauty" (28:17).

18. "Thou hast corrupted thy *wisdom* by reason of thy brightness" (28:17).

19. "I will cast thee to the ground" (28:17).

Compare "I beheld Satan as lightning fall from heaven" (Jesus).

Here are at least *eighteen* things said of Tyrus which certainly seem to look beyond him or any other person or place, to Satan, the devil, who was undoubtedly the first sinner in the universe of God. Created a white-winged, perfect and beautiful musical cherub, he rebelled against his Creator and Preserver and became the black-winged monster of iniquity now known as the devil and Satan.

They shall know that I am the Lord (28:23).

This is one of the key expressions of the Book of Ezekiel. God's dealings with Jews and Gentiles alike are in order to bring them to their senses and a realization of God. His punishments of His people, His just indignation against the Gentile nations is in order that they might know that the Lord is God in heaven above and in the earth beneath.

KEY
"This is Pharaoh and all his multitude" (31:18)

21

THE DOOM OF EGYPT

EZEKIEL 29-32

Ezekiel 29 to 32 deals with Pharaoh and Egypt (type of Satan and this present evil world). Nebuchadnezzar's sin reached its height and limit in his pompous boast about Babylon, and Pharaoh's folly reached its finale when he said, "The river is mine, and I have made it" (29:9). What insanity and imbecility. What madness and folly for any mere man to say, *this is mine* and what wickedness to declare, *I have made it.* "I" in the place of God and mine instead of "His." What pomp and pride can possess the mind and heart of man. "This is Pharaoh and all his multitude."

The basest of the kingdoms (29:15).

"And I will bring again the captivity of Egypt, and will cause them to return into the land of Pathros, into the land of their habitation, and they shall be there a base kingdom. It shall be the basest of the kingdoms; neither shall it exalt itself any more above the nations: for I will diminish them, that they shall no more rule over the nations" (29:14, 15).

These words were uttered when Pharaoh and Egypt were in their glory and grandeur. God knows the end from the beginning and through the Prophet

Ezekiel made known that He would make the land utterly waste and desolate from Seveneh to Ethiopia. "They shall be a base kingdom." "It shall be the basest of the kingdoms." "Neither shall it exalt itself any more above the nations." How completely these prophecies have been fulfilled and how fully and minutely fulfilling to this day is known to every student of the past and present. Egypt *was* the pride and glory of the Gentile world. Egypt *is* now a base, low kingdom. Egypt *was* amongst the most prosperous and pompous of empires. Egypt *is now* the basest of kingdoms. Prophecy is simply history foretold. God's frown was a chill of death to Pharaoh and Egypt and is a precursor of doom and damnation to all who follow their own pernicious ways. The Egyptians of today may strike and fight for independence and a restoration of their past status, power and glory, but it is all in vain. The outcome was all made known 2,500 years ago. Egypt shall no more rule over the nations. Egypt shall no more exalt itself above the nations. Egypt shall be a base kingdom (29:14, 15). The divine *fiat* has gone forth *and* so it is.

The greatness, grandeur and glory of old Egypt is set forth by one writer in the following glowing terms: "Such vast and surprising remains are still to be seen of such magnificence and solidity as may convince anyone who beholds them that without some extraordinary accident they must have lasted forever." Nothing short of an unusual catastrophe can possible account for the ruination of Egypt. Twenty-five hundred years ago Jeremiah was inspired to pen the following lines: "Go up into Gilead and take balm, O virgin daughter of Egypt; in vain dost thou use medicines. There is no healing for thee." How did the preacher know? How could the prophet foretell? After twenty-five centuries, Egypt is still sick and the British government is now its new nurse. It was not to be destroyed entirely; it was to be sick. How could Jeremiah or Ezekiel know the future history of Egypt? Egypt is sick today, weak today, being nursed today. Great Britain is the nurse and there is no healing. Neither Britain, nor Italy, nor Egypt can make her well. Hear these words of the inspired penmen and then read history and you will find that prophecy is simply history foretold. Speaking of Egypt, "I will diminish *them.... They* shall no more rule over the nations.... *Her* foundations shall be broken up.... The pride of *her* power shall come down" (Ezek. 29: 15; 30: 4; 30: 6). At the time of this prophecy Egypt was a world power and in her glory. Where is she now? Read the Bible and the newspaper and believe. Has Egypt been diminished? Are they ruling now over the nations? Have her foundations been broken up? Has the pride of her power come down?

Egypt is now a base kingdom, exactly as Jeremiah and Ezekiel foretold (Ezek. 29: 14). The pyramids of Egypt are still the wonder of the world. The sphinx of Egypt is still a puzzle and an enigma to students.

Egypt . . . shall be the wages for his . . . labour (29: 19, 20).

God is just and righteous to both sinner and saint, prince and peasant. He pays wages to all His servants either in the present or future. Nebuchadnezzar was God's chosen rod to punish the sinful and proud Tyrus and everything was so utterly consumed that the conqueror (Nebuchadnezzar) obtained no spoil (no wages). Now the cup of iniquity was overflowing for Egypt. Egypt's day of doom had dawned and the treasures of Egypt were to be given to Nebuchadnezzar as wages for him and his army for service against Tyrus. God is righteous in all His ways, and holy in all His works. God remains a debtor to neither men nor angels, sinners nor saints. Nebuchadnezzar was God's hireling and God paid him good wages.

The day of the Lord is near

It is simply impossible to read these 32 chapters of Ezekiel and then conclude that they have reached their complete fulfillment in the past. These prophecies look beyond Egypt, Tyre and Jerusalem of the past to a future "day of the Lord" and a future judgment upon Jerusalem (God's city) and a future Egypt (the world).

These predictions look beyond Pharaoh, the prince of Tyrus, and the wicked, profane prince Zedekiah to another king and prince (Satan) and to another profane prince (Antichrist) and to another far worse "day of the Lord," even the tribulation *the great*. These are all foreshadowings of the last days. "The day of the Lord is near." Man's day of sin and wrong has lasted almost 6,000 years, and we are persuaded that God's day, God's seventh day of millennial rest will soon be ushered in, and wrong and sin shall be put upon the scaffold and holiness placed upon the throne. God, haste the happy day!

I cast him down to hell (31: 16).

Pharaoh and Egypt were comparable to Nebuchadnezzar and Babylon. Like a cedar for strength, height and majesty, and planted beside great waters, prosperous and influential and with limitless possibilities of blessing to mankind, Pharaoh and his people became proud in heart and haughty in head until their cup of wickedness overflowed and God Almighty in fury and hate cast them down to hell. Hell is here defined by the divine penman himself as the nether part of the earth. *Not* the grave (which is but six feet below the surface)—as the ranting and ridiculous Russellites and Rutherfordites teach and try to believe—but the *nether parts* of the earth. The grave receives the body, while Sheol—the nether *parts* of the earth—receives the soul. "I will cast him down to hell." I will bring him down to the abode of the dead and damned—the unseen regions of doom and despair. What folly to try to make these words of warning mean the grave, for the grave will receive us all, if Jesus tarries. Pharaoh and Philip, Paul and Pilate alike are in the grave as far as the body is concerned, but Paul is in Paradise above and Pilate in perdition below. Pharaoh is writhing in the flames of a self-chosen hell while Philip is walking along Hallelujah Avenue in Heaven. The grave receives only that which is material and Sheol receives that which is immaterial and eternal.

I will cover the sun with a cloud (32:7).

For Pharaoh and Egypt, a dreadful day was predicted. Pharaoh was likened to a fierce, dangerous, terrifying young lion, and also likened to a huge dragon in the seas, stirring up the dirt, disturbing the nations and corrupting mankind.

God's net was to be spread and he was to be taken and miserably destroyed. The heavens were to put on sackcloth, the sun was to be covered with a cloud and the moon was to be so shocked it would refuse to look upon the devastation and desolation. The stars in dismay would hide their faces and a black mantle of dense darkness would cover the earth.

All nature is in harmony with God and in sympathy with her Creator. The heavens above and the earth beneath are in harmony with God and holiness. Only man is vile. Ever and anon floods unleash their fury and cover the earth, sweeping its sinful inhabitants from the face of the ground. The sun will stand still to assure a holy Joshua of complete triumph in the extermination of sin. The earth gladly opens its jaws in order to swallow the critical Korahs and the damnable Dathans. Nature will gladly sing a funeral dirge at the departure of God haters, Christ rejecters, and holiness fighters, for nature is God's handmaid.

Their iniquities shall be upon their bones (32:27).

Sin makes an indelible mark upon the body, soul, heart and mind of man. The soul of man is its own recording secretary and stenographer. The very contemplation of sin will cause the heart to beat faster and the sensitive organ will palpitate its refusal to condone impurity and sin.

The blood stream will increase its steady flow and the blood will increase its own temperature at the very contemplation of wrong until the head and hand will tingle a bell of warning against wickedness.

Sin makes an indelible mark and leaves its lasting impression even upon the bones. To commit sin is to commit suicide.

I will judge you every one after his ways (33:20).

Divine equity in the Divine dealings with everyone is assured. Ezekiel chapter 33 sets forth:

1. The duty of the watchman.
2. The challenge of an unchanging God.
3. The fulfillment of a prophecy.

I. THE DUTY OF A WATCHMAN
    1. To watch while others sleep.
    2. To fix the attention while others are listless.

3. To warn by blowing the trumpet.
4. To awaken by sounding an alarm.

II. THE CHALLENGE OF GOD

"Say unto them, As I live, saith the Lord God, I have no pleasure in the death of the wicked; but that the wicked turn from his way and live: turn ye, turn ye from your evil ways; for why will ye die, O house of Israel?"

III. THE FULFILLMENT OF A PROPHECY

"And it came to me in the twelfth year of our captivity, in the tenth month, in the fifth day of the month, that one that had escaped out of Jerusalem came unto me, saying, The city is smitten."

PROPHECY FULFILLED
KEY: "The city is smitten" (33:21)

22

THE CITY IS SMITTEN

EZEKIEL 33-36

The city is smitten

Isaiah was the *evangelical* prophet of *faith*. Jeremiah was the *weeping* prophet of *love,* and Ezekiel was the *exiled* prophet of *hope*.

Year after year he preached, prophesied and performed. His miniature siege of Jerusalem, the shaving of his hair and beard, the escape from the hole in the wall, the sudden death of his wife, the pictures of the doom and the destruction of Jerusalem—each and all fell upon deaf ears. The stiff-necked people to whom he preached and about whom he prophesied and before whom he performed refused to believe his word and profit by his message until one of the fleeing refugees came with the sad news, "The city is smitten." God and Ezekiel warned that it would be smitten and now the message, "The city *is* smitten."

He shall ... die (33: 18).

For the third time in this book of prophecy the Holy Ghost warns that it is possible for a holy man to sin and lose his soul. With these plain truths before us argument is useless. The debate is closed.

1. "The righteousness of the righteous shall not deliver him in the day of his transgression" (v. 12).

2. "Neither shall the righteous be able to live ... in the day that he sinneth" (v. 12).

127

3. "When I shall say to the righteous, that he shall surely live; if he trust to his own righteousness and commit iniquity, all his righteousnesses shall not be remembered; but for his iniquity that he hath committed, he shall die for it" (v. 13).

4. "When the righteous turneth from his righteousness, and committeth iniquity, he shall even die thereby" (v. 18).

My mouth was opened (33: 22).

God had spoken through the prophet and he had faithfully and fearlessly warned His people and delivered his own soul. God then sealed the lips of His servant.

Both princes and people alike refused to give heed to the ringing bells of warning, the judgments of Jehovah mercilessly swept over Jerusalem and the Jews were massacred and murdered by the madmen of Babylon. Then the mouth of the prophet was opened and the word of God doubly fulfilled. "One that had escaped out of Jerusalem came unto me saying, The city is smitten." God through the Prophet Ezekiel had predicted the smiting of the city and *seven* years later one who escaped out of the city of Jerusalem came unto Ezekiel saying, "The city is smitten." God's word is certain, steadfast, infallible and sure.

They hear . . . but they will not do (33: 31).

"And, lo, thou art unto them as a very lovely song of one that hath a pleasant voice, and can play well on an instrument: for they hear thy words, but they do them not." What an indictment! Hearing but not doing. Knowing but not profited. Informed but also inactive. If each person on earth would do what he now knows to be right and leave alone that which he now knows to be wrong, doubtful or questionable, a revival such as the world or church has never witnessed would break out like a prairie fire, hell would be defeated, Satan sidetracked and heaven enlarged. The damning sin of our day is the sin of *knowing* but not doing. It is not information that people need but the willingness to do the right as they now know it. It is not *light* that is needed but a walking in the light which is already possessed. The trouble with sinful, unbelieving men is not Cain's wife but some other wife or something that they want worse than they want the will of God. The trouble is not in the head but in the heart. The stumbling block is not in the brain but in the sinful, wilful, stubborn soul. The trouble is not Jonah and the whale but the unwillingness to do the will of God which they now know. The damning sin of our day is hearing but not doing.

I am against the shepherds (34:10).

Chapter 34 of Ezekiel administers a sharp, scathing reproof of selfish shepherds.

1. Woe be to the shepherds . . . that do feed themselves!"

2. "The diseased have ye not strengthened."

3. "Neither have ye healed that which was sick."

4. "Neither have ye bound up that which was broken."

5. "Neither have ye brought again that which was driven away."

6. "Neither have ye sought that which was lost."

7. "Behold . . . I will require my flock at their hand."

The hottest spot in perdition will be that occupied by unfaithful and insincere preachers.

I . . . will strengthen then that which was sick (34: 16).

"I will . . . seek them out" (v. 11).

"I will . . . deliver them" (v. 12).

"I will bring them out" (v. 13).

"I will bring . . . them in" (v. 13).

"I will feed them" (v. 14).

"I will cause them to lie down" (v. 15).

"I will . . . bind up the broken" (v. 16).

"I will . . . strengthen the sick" (v. 16).

I have heard (35:13).

Mount Seir was the dwelling place of the Edomites, the descendants of Esau. The Israelites were the descendants of Jacob, and Esau hated Jacob. The hatred of Esau against Jacob was handed down to all future generations. The Edomites were a pleasure loving, selfish, soup sipping, hog eating, proud, insolent set of boasters and blasphemers.

God Almighty was not only against them, but gives the reason for their removal and ruin (35: 5, 6).

The Book of Numbers (20:14-21) gives an interesting sidelight upon the conduct of the Edomites, while God's people were pressing their way to the promised land. Perpetual hatred burned in the heart of the Edomites. They had murdered the children of Jacob in the time when they needed mercy and help. In their hearts they coveted the land of Palestine for themselves, and but for the goodness of God, not an Israelite would have remained alive. Such hellish hatred finally produced a Herod and will finally produce the coming Antichrist. Jacob's choice ended in the Christ of Calvary and the redemption of the race, while Esau's hatred ended in the coming of a hateful Herod and the soon coming of the yet more abominable Antichrist. The end of Esau's hatred is not yet.

The Lord God, looking down into the unborn centuries and seeing the polluting stream from the hateful Esau, said, "Esau have I hated," and seeing the end of Jacob's faith and choice in the stable of Bethlehem said, "Jacob have I loved." The sin and selfishness of the one culminated in the cruel Herod, while the vision and heart throb for God in Jacob culminated in the Christ of Bethlehem, and the cross of Calvary.

Flocks of men (36:37).

"The flock of my pasture, *are* men" (34:31).

The 36th chapter of Ezekiel is a pure oasis in the desert of judgments and punishments prophesied in this Book of Ezekiel.

It contains a glowing prediction and promise of Israel's restoration to their own land, their cleansing from sin and idolatry and their entire sanctification by the baptism with the Holy Spirit (also prophesied by Joel and partially fulfilled on the day of Pentecost), after which they shall become worldwide missionaries, for the heathen shall know.

"And I will sanctify my great name, which was profaned among the heathen, which ye have profaned in the midst of them; and the heathen shall know that I am the Lord, saith the Lord God when I shall be sanctified in you before their eyes."

The land that was desolate shall become like the Garden of Eden and through the Jew—restored, reclaimed, regenerated and filled with the Holy Ghost—all mankind shall be blessed.

I will increase them with men like a flock (36:37).

In answer to prevailing prayer and a persistent pleading of the promises of God, *revival* is gloriously possible.

"Thus saith the Lord God; I will yet for this be inquired of by the house of Israel, to do it for them, I will increase them with men like a flock."

1. CONVERSION (v. 24).
   (1) "I will take you from"
   (2) "and gather you out"

2. Regeneration (vs. 25, 26).
   (1) "Outward cleansing (v. 25).
   (2) "Inward renewing" (v. 26, first clause).

3. Entire Sanctification (vs. 26, 27).
   (1) Heart cleansing.
      "I will take away the stony heart" (v. 26).
   (2) Fullness of the Spirit.
      "I will put my Spirit within you" (v. 27).
   (3) Power.
      "and cause you to walk—and keep—and do" (v. 27).
   (4) Prosperity and plenty (vs. 29, 30).
      "I will call for the corn" (v. 29).
      "I will multiply the fruit" (v. 30).
   (5) Evangelization of the world.
      "The heathen shall know . . . when I am sanctified in you before their eyes" (v. 23).

The Vision of the Very Dry Bones (37:1-14)
KEY: "Son of man, these bones are the whole
house of Israel" (37:11)

23

VISION OF DRY BONES

Can these bones live? (37:3).

The Lord's hand was upon Ezekiel and he was carried in the spirit, and set down in the midst of a valley of very dry bones. Having set down the prophet in the midst of such chilling surroundings, the Lord propounded the question, "Can these bones live?" Can *these* bones live? Can these *bones* live? Can these bones *live?*

The prophet was commanded to preach to the dry bones, and, always implicit and unquestioning in his obedience, the prophet calls upon the bones to hear the word of the Lord.

Suddenly there was *a noise,* then a shaking and the bones came together—head and arm to shoulder, rib to spine and ankle to limb—bone by bone. Flesh came upon the bones and skin covered the flesh, but there was no breath in them.

The prophet was commissioned to prophesy unto the wind and call the four winds to breathe upon the dead bodies that they might live. The prophet obeyed and the breath of God came into the dead bodies and they lived and jumped to their feet an exceeding great army.

The meaning is plain.

1. The bones *are* the children of Israel.
2. The graves *are* the Gentile nations.

3. Israel shall be restored to their own land as from the dead.

"Then he said unto me, Son of man, these bones are the whole house of Israel; behold they say, Our bones are dried, and our hope is lost; we are cut off for our parts. Therefore prophesy and say unto them, Thus saith the Lord God; Behold, O my people, I will open your graves, and cause you to come up out of your graves, and bring you into the land of Israel. And ye shall know that I am the Lord, when I have opened your graves, O my people, and brought you up out of your graves. And shall put my spirit in you, and ye shall live; and I shall place you in your own land: then shall ye know that I the Lord have spoken it, and performed it, saith the Lord."

The Two Sticks (37: 15-28).

I will save them and will cleanse them (37: 23).

The symbol of the two sticks, one for Judah and the half tribe of Benjamin and the other for Israel including the double portion for Joseph, to be joined together, become one, with one king over them—having been saved and sanctified, foreshadows the coming millennium.

Ten things are promised:

1. Israel and Judah united (two sticks) (v. 19).
2. Saved (v. 23).
3. Cleansed (v. 23).
4. Restored (v. 24).
5. Obedient (v. 24).

6. A new king (v. 25).
7. Peace (v. 26).
8. Worship restored (v. 27).
9. Again the Chosen People (v. 27).
10. Blessing to all mankind (v. 28).

Jehovah, through the prophet, had already announced the restoration of the nation and now gives in vision and symbol the method of its sure fulfillment.

(1) The *bones* are the living Israelites. (2) The *graves* are the nations among whom they dwell. (3) The *two sticks* are Judah and Israel. (4) United, one nation, the twelve tribes.

THE END OF THE AGE
KEY: "It shall be in the latter days"

24

IN THE LATTER DAYS

EZEKIEL 38

The Ruin of Russia (38:1-4).
The Inevitable Collapse of Italy (38:5-7).
The Defeat and Destruction of Germany Prophesied
   (Ezekiel 38:6-13).

It is now Saturday, September 21, 1940. It is too early to judge correctly the final outcome of the present conflict between Germany and England, but when almost everyone is expecting England to be defeated and Germany with Italy to win the war this scribe ventures an opinion. With the Bible now open before his eyes at Ezekiel 38 and 39 this writer thinks that the Gog of Ezekiel 38:2 is the ruler, prince or dictator of Russia, that the Magog of verse 2 is the land and people of Russia, that Meshech and Tubal represent the present Moscow and Tobolsk, and that God is definitely against them (v. 3); that Russia will be ruinously defeated (v. 4); that Italy will lose Ethiopia and Libya (v. 5); that Germany will be badly beaten and finally split up into small states or bands (v. 6), and that all who co-operate with Germany and Italy will finally fail and fall, i.e., "many people with thee" (38:6).

In the spring of this year, just before the collapse of France and when everything seemed hopeless and Great Britain seemed certainly doomed, scores of people, preachers and leaders asked how the war was coming out, to which I consistently replied, "All right. Great Britain will win." This reply was based on what I believed to be the solid rock of Scripture. It is now September 21 and while the situation seems hopeless, I am still convinced that Great Britain will win with the help of our own United States and that the whole nasty business will shape up toward the end days of Ezekiel 38 and 39.

Germany was to come *like a storm*, i.e., suddenly, and sweep everything before her (38:9), and hence the word *blitzkrieg*. Such is clearly stated in verse nine of Ezekiel thirty-eight. The very word *storm*, i.e., lightning, is used in the Scripture and the newspapers have been filled with the German blitzkrieg or lightning war; God knows the end from the beginning.

The German ruler or dictator was to think an evil thought (v. 10), or conceive a mischievous purpose (v. 10, margin). He was to decide an attack on England and Palestine. An invasion of Holland, Denmark, Norway and England was to be carefully planned and promptly executed (vs. 11, 12). Germany and her allies are to be defeated by God Almighty. Pestilence, hail, rain, lightning and flood would stop the onward march of the legions of hell (38:2).

The whole world, including England, shall yet be judged and suffer for their sins (39:1-6). Palestine shall be protected and Israel finally restored, redeemed and sanctified (38: 29).

The present conflict is a shadow of things to come. Great Britain with our United States, under God, while suffering severely, will triumph. Germany will be defeated and divided into numerous small states and bands. Italy will lose her African possessions of Ethiopia and Libya especially, and the path cleared for the final drama, a last world conflict.

God Almighty had the first word (Gen. 1: 3), and God shall have the last word (Ezekiel 39: 29 and 48: 35).

The present horrors of war, as diabolical and hellish as they are, will seem like a Sunday school picnic compared to the final clash and cataclysmic judgments of the oncoming last days.

When God arises to judge the earth, woe to the war lords of all the earth, woe to the Christ rejecters, holiness despisers and God haters of every land.

Set thy face against Gog (38: 2).

Gog and Magog were the children of Japheth. The word Gog means *king* and Magog means kingly people (nobility). This prophecy is yet to be fulfilled. These two chapters are a prediction of the Great Tribulation *after* the Rapture of the saints, and *before* the return of Christ to reign as King. Without dogmatizing on predictions yet to be fulfilled, and not wishing to venture where angels fear to tread, and not being a prophet nor the son of a prophet in the Old Testament sense of the word, we venture to suggest that these verses may refer to the great Northern Empire of Russia.

Meshech and Tubal (38: 3) may be Moscow and Tobolsk. Persia, Ethiopia and Lybia are yet with us (v. 5) and Gomer (v. 6) and all his bands may take in Germany, and the reference to "them that dwell confidently in the isles" (39: 6) may take in the whole of Great Britain such as England, Ireland, Scotland, Wales.

These two chapters predict a confederacy of nations against Israel and it is possible that in the final battle of Armageddon, Russia, Germany, Japan and India with others shall unite their forces against Israel and Israel's God. The earth shall quake and tremble under the feet of marching millions of mad monarchs and men.

The sickening end of man's day is seen in verses 17-22.

Behold, I am against thee, O God (38: 3).

The prophet has undoubtedly in mind the northern powers headed by Russia. The prince is Gog and the land and people Magog while Meshech and Tubal are Moscow and Tobolsk. The whole prophecy looks forward to the Great Tribulation, the battle of Armageddon and still forward to the final rebellion at the close of the millennium.

PART FOUR
Conversion and Worship of Restored Israel

25

THE MILLENNIUM

EZEKIEL 40-47:8

The Millennial Temple.

I. DESCRIPTION OF THE TEMPLE (40-43).
1. The Vision (40:1-4).
2. The Eastern Gate (5-16).
3. The Outer Court (17-27).
4. The Inner Court (28-38).
5. The Tables and Chambers (39-47).
6. The Porch (48, 49).
7. The Holy Place (41:1, 2).
8. The Holy of Holies (3, 4).
9. The Interior Decorations (5-26).
10. The Priests' Chambers (42:1-14).
11. The Final Measurements (15-20).
12. The Glory of the Lord returns and fills the house (43:1-6).
13. The Law of the House (Holiness) (13-17).

II. THE WORSHIP OF THE TEMPLE (43-46).
1. The Offerings (43:18-27).
2. The Prince and Priests (44:1-31; 45:1-17).
3. The Feasts (45:18-25).
4. The Worship of Prince and people (46:1-24).

III. THE LAND AND THE CITY (47, 48).
1. The Living Waters (47:1-12).
2. The Borders of the Land (13-21).

3. The Stranger in the Land (22, 23).
4. The Portions of the Tribes (48: 1-29).
5. The Gates of the City and its new name, (Jehovah-Shammah (48: 1-29).

With profound thankfulness to God for His marvelous mercy and gracious goodness to usward we conclude this brief exposition of the Book of Ezekiel.

Set me upon a very high mountain (40: 2).

The pattern for the Tabernacle and its altar was given to Moses on the Mount. The plans for the Temple of Solomon and its courts were given to David and the pattern and plans of the Millennial Temple were given to Ezekiel, the prophet of the Lord.

The man with the measuring reed suggests that everything is to be in harmony with every other part and *all* by Divine appointment and finished according to the Divine Will.

The *seven* steps, while actual steps in an actual temple may suggest the necessity of

1. Conviction
2. Repentance.
3. Faith.
4. Regeneration.
5. Testimony.
6. Consecration.
7. Sanctification (40: 22).

The *eight* steps (vs. 31, 34, 37) may also suggest our glorification at the Second Coming of Christ thus completing the new man, spirit, soul and body.

The chambers of the singers may intimate the happy and hilarious hours spent in holy worship in this holy temple (40: 44).

The spaciousness and magnificence of this Millennial Temple amazes the devout mind of the reader and student. It baffles description. The law of the house shall be holiness (43: 12). Wise, ordained and anointed teachers shall rightly divide the word of truth (44: 23). Tithes and offerings for the support of the ministry shall be faithfully presented before the Lord (44: 29, 30). All shall give as God prospers. Holiness campmeetings shall be held every six months and atonement made every morning for mistakes, short-comings and continued life and health. Living waters shall flow freely and abundantly in every direction. Meat shall be found on fruitful trees and medicine from healthful leaves and mankind shall at last be privileged to drink from the fountain of youth for "The Lord is there."

The concluding chapters of Ezekiel describe the Millennial Temple.

The offerings look *back* to a finished redemption on Calvary, as the Levitical offerings looked *forward*. All salvation is in Christ. The Lord's Supper is *now* a memorial of a completed redemption by Christ, as the offerings and sacrifices connected with the temple in the Millennium will be memorial offerings and sacrifices. The cross of Christ stands in the center separating Abel and Genesis from the sons of Zadok in the Millennial Temple. Abel looked *forward* in *faith*, while the sons of Zadok will look *back* to a *fact*, the fact of redemption through Christ. It is instructive to notice:

1. No evening sacrifices are mentioned as these were done away in the sacrifice of Christ.

2. The feast of Pentecost is not mentioned as that is fulfilled in this dispensation.

3. No evening lamb is mentioned as the night of sin is gone forever.

A measuring reed (40:3).

He who measures the oceans in the hollow of His hand, who piled up the mountains and scooped out the valleys, who meted out the heavens with a span and weighed the dust of the whole earth with a balance, who numbers His people and also numbers the hairs of their heads, who governs the movements and motions of the suns, moons and stars, also has a measure for the New Temple in which He is to be worshiped.

The first measurement given in the Bible was for the ark which was to be prepared by Noah. The second measurement was for the Ark of the Covenant, which was shown to Moses on the Mount after which followed the measurements for the Mercy Seat, the Table of Shewbread, the details of the Tabernacle ending with the Golden Altar of Incense.

He also gave to David the pattern of the Temple and of every detail, in weight and also in measurement. These were all dwelling places for the Most Holy.

1. The Ark made by Noah.
2. The Tabernacle built by Moses.
3. The Temple erected by Solomon.
4. The Millennial Temple.

God does not dwell in anything, anywhere, any place and anyhow. There must be preparation, order and proportion.

In the selfsame day (40: 10).

The tenth day of the month was a notable day in all Israel. It was on that selfsame day each household took a lamb, to be kept till the 14th day, when, by the shed blood of the lamb they were sheltered from the judgment of Jehovah (see Exodus 12).

It was on that selfsame day some forty years later that the Lord did wonders among them and the waters divided in Jordan and they passed through as on dry land (see Joshua 3: 5).

It was also on that selfsame day that the Lord did curse the barren fig tree, saying unto it, "No man eat fruit of thee for ever." It was on the tenth day of the month that the Lord vouchsafed to Ezekiel the glory and grandeur of this coming Millennial Temple.

And the glory came into the house (43:4).

Ezekiel saw the glory of God slowly but surely depart

    (1) From the cherubim,

    (2) From the threshold,

    (3) From the temple and,

    (4) From the city, and now he beholds its return.

And the glory filled the house (43:5).

    (1) The glory *departed* from the house.

    (2) The glory *returned* to the house.

    (3) The glory *filled* the house.

A sin offering (43:19).

These offerings will be memorial offerings looking back to the cross of Calvary as the Levitical offerings looked forward. In the Sacrament of the Lord's Supper we look back to a finished redemption and forward to Christ's coming again. In the offerings and sacrifices described and depicted by Ezekiel there is the backward glance at Calvary and the forward look to the Prince and the glory of God filling the house.

The sons of Zadok (44:15).

Chapters 40 to 48 may be divided into three almost equal parts.

    1. The Temple proper (40-42).

    2. The worship (43-46).

    3. The land and city (47, 48).

The sons of Zadok were especially faithful to God in times of special unfaithfulness and unbelief and are given special honor in the Millennial Temple worship.

They shall be clothed with linen garments (44:17).

The priestly sons of the devout and faithful Zadok were to be special ministers unto the Lord.

Linen and not woolen garments were to be worn. Wool is obtained from animals and causes irritation and sweat. Sweat is the result of sin. "In the sweat of thy face shalt thou eat bread until," was part of the sentence passed upon Adam. Nothing that savored of sin was to be allowed in the presence of God.

Linen garments (holy life), linen bonnets (submission to God and each other), linen breeches (holy walk), were allowed, but nothing was permitted that caused sweat (v. 18).

The Vision of the Living Waters (Ezekiel 47)

Living—ever-flowing—overflowing — fruit producing—beautifying waters flowed from the threshold of the temple. Trees with abundant leaves and fruit beautified the river and made glad the garden of God. The fruit of the trees was for meat, and the leaves for medicine.

The Millennial City with this majestic, awe-inspiring, God-planned Millennial Temple will be named Jehovah-Shammah, which means "the Lord is there." The concluding two chapters form a fitting climax to this profound book of prophecy. Beginning with a glowing description of the glory of the Lord, then *the glory* slowly and hesitatingly departing, followed by judgments upon Jerusalem in particular, and the Gentiles in general, *then* the messages of hope and comfort to the sorrowing remnant, followed by a detailed description of Israel's return, restoration and salvation, the final conflicts, the returning glory of the Lord, the Millennial City and Temple and "The Lord is There."

The city through which he walked with tired feet became the glorious footstool of His Majesty, *The King*. Long live the King. "The Lord is there."

A spiritual interpretation of Ezekiel forty-seven does not satisfy the student of sacred Scripture. While the increasing depths of water undoubtedly has its symbolic significance it does not exhaust this superb chapter of the sacred and sublime volume.

It is interesting to note that in our own day a chemical analysis of the Dead Sea has placed a value of its contents as exceeding one thousand billion dollars. That is $500 for every human on earth to-day, and it is an amount equaling in value *three* United States of America. As certainly as we now pen these lines a mammoth concern of chemical companies will some day empty the Dead Sea of its enormous treasure and the Dead Sea will be "healed."

These waters go down to the desert (47:8).

Not only will these chapters be literally fulfilled to the children of Abraham in the flesh, but they have practical and spiritual lessons to the children of Abraham in the Spirit, the children of faith.

1. The river is a fitting type of the descent of the Holy Spirit (Holiness).

2. The living waters to the ankles (holy walk).

3. The waters to the knees (holy worship).

4. Waters to the loins (holy service).

5. Waters in which to swim (holy life in ever-increasing and enlarging circles of usefulness, and blessing) even into the desert (the regions beyond).

26

EVERLASTING LIFE, HEALTH AND HAPPINESS

EZEKIEL 47

Everything shall live whither the river cometh (Ezek. 47:9).

Sin brought death into the world of mankind. Man begins to die as soon as he is born. Sickness, disease and sorrow have filled the earth with broken hearts and bodies. The ground under our feet is hollow with graves of the dead and the air around is tremulous with the groans of the suffering and dying. Satan and sin, disease and death are rampant in the streets of cities and in the lanes and homes of the villages of every land. The pale horse and his rider reaps a fearful harvest and hell follows close upon his heels. Thank God! there is to dawn a better day. Christ is not only the Way and the Truth but He is the Life, and in one of God's tomorrows sin shall be swept from the earth, Satan shall be shut up in hell forever and Holiness shall ascend the throne of the universe, and life, health, holiness and happiness shall be the order of the day. The heart of this writer says, "Even so, come Lord Jesus."

The leaf . . . for medicine (47:12).

"And by the river upon the bank thereof, on this side and on that side, shall grow all trees for meat, whose leaf shall not fade, neither shall the fruit thereof be consumed; it shall bring forth new fruit according to his months, because their waters they issued out of the sanctuary; and the fruit thereof shall be for meat, and the leaf for medicine (47:12).

A clear understanding of the Millennium and Millennium days will help the reader to a better understanding of the Bible as a whole. The word Millennium means a thousand years, and refers to that coming period of time when Christ shall be King in Jerusalem and when the saints with Him shall rule the earth. The Millennium will not be a perfect state or period. The human family will live in the flesh or body, just as we do now, but without the activity and temptations of a personal devil. Satan will be arrested at the close of the Great Tribulation and chained in the Bottomless Pit, but babies will be born with carnality—devil nature—in them. The law of Christ, and stern rule with the rod of iron, will keep sin in check, but carnality is not subject to any law of God or man, and sin will break out in divers places to be instantly punished by Millennial police and detectives. No man will be allowed to commit sin without instant arrest and punishment. All laws will be strictly enforced. Having dealt fully with these millennial conditions and truths elsewhere we here conclude by reminding the reader that babies will be born during the Millennium just as they are now—minus the lust and aggravation of the devil. Learning to walk, many of them will fall, bruise their little bodies and skin their shins and hence the need of medicine, millennial medicine.

"The fruit thereof shall be for meat" for man shall become a vegetarian again and "the leaf thereof for bruises and sores."

The Millennium will be on the earth. It will not be an ideal state. Perfect conditions will not prevail. The inhabitants will make *mistakes* and hence the need of offerings and sacrifices for atonement. They will also need meat and hence the need of trees for fruit. They will need water and hence the need of living water everywhere and they will need medicine to keep them well, healthful and strong. No one will die except through transgression of the known laws of Christ.

The God intended age limit of man will be reached and enjoyed for the first time in human history, for holiness shall be on the throne and sin shall be on the scaffold. Christ shall be Supreme Dictator, King and Lord.